Amazing disgrace

Amazing disgrace

A BOOK ABOUT "SHAME"

GRACE CAMPBELL

HODDER studio

First published in Great Britain in 2020 by Hodder Studio
An Hachette UK company

1

Copyright © Grace Campbell 2020

Illustrations by Alice Skinner

A CIP catalogue record for this title is available from the British Library

Hardback ISBN 9781529354003
eBook ISBN 9781529354010

Typeset in Sabon LT by Hewer Text UK Ltd, Edinburgh
Printed and bound in Great Britain by Clays Ltd, Elcograf S.p.A.

Hodder & Stoughton policy is to use papers that are natural, renewable and recyclable products and made from wood grown in sustainable forests. The logging and manufacturing processes are expected to conform to the environmental regulations of the country of origin.

Hodder & Stoughton Ltd
Carmelite House
50 Victoria Embankment
London EC4Y 0DZ

www.hodder-studio.com

For Tyler,

You are magic. Thanks for putting up with me.
For always answering the phone, no matter
what time it is.

Lylas (Love you like a sister)

INTRODUCTION

The thing is, I first felt ashamed of my vagina when I had my first wank. I was seven. Now, I'm a competitive person – I love coming first – so I'm glad that I beat my friends to this milestone. But of course I didn't know what a wank was then, so I couldn't even brag about it.

It all happened innocently enough. I was lying in bed one night, drifting off to sleep, when I got this light, fluttery feeling in my vagina, a bit like butterflies, and instinctively I knew I had to see to it like it was a delivery man at the front door. What arrived was an urgent need to hump something. Of all my unsuspecting teddy bears, I chose Toby, who was conveniently in bed with me. Toby looked like a Tory. He had the smug face of someone who's just done a fart and got away with it, and he wore one of those thin woollen scarves that only people who were in the Bullingdon Club wear. I humped Toby the Tory teddy until I reached a feeling of pure ecstasy. It was the best feeling I'd ever experienced. It reminded me of the time I first tried Maltesers. My insides felt glittery, and I felt like if I closed my eyes, I could levitate.

But that feeling quickly subsided and then I instantly became paralysed with shame. I hated myself for doing what I'd done – I thought it was so bad that if anyone found out, I'd be arrested and sent to Alcatraz, which I had

3

just heard of from a boy in my class whose dad was American. I thought I'd be kicked out of my school for being so perverse. Should I put Toby under the bed? He certainly wasn't going to any more teddy bears' picnics. I couldn't look at him, the posh pervert.

I have no idea where that feeling of shame came from. I really don't know why I didn't run downstairs and excitedly tell my mum that I had just discovered the most marvellous thing. I should have been so proud that I had found wanking without anyone telling me about it. I was a pioneer! But some part of me knew that this wasn't something I should talk about. This was an act that I should keep between me and my vag. Us two were in this together. Shame or no shame.

After that first time, I kept doing it – a lot. That short moment of pleasure was worth it. So many things made me want to do it. Arthur the aardvark. Draco Malfoy. Kim Kardashian's sex tape, which I saw when I was eleven. The coach in *Bend It Like Beckham*. Usher. Chad Michael Murray. Jesse Metcalfe and Eva Longoria in *Desperate Housewives*. Seth Cohen. I developed a secret sexual relationship with myself and the people that turned me on. And as my ability to give myself orgasms continued, the more I started to feel like a disgrace.

I hoped this shameful feeling would go away when I finally had sex. I thought that once sex happened, I'd feel like all of the adults I'd been wanking to. I'd be like Kim

Kardashian. But when I started having sex, a new kind of shame arrived. Shame that I was doing everything wrong. Shame that my vagina was a scientific anomaly that no one would ever be able to understand. Shame that I would never be good at sex because I'd been humping things for too long. Shame that I would one day accidentally fanny fart so hard the dick would come out . . . That one came true. More on that later . . .

And although I had been practising my wanking skills like a competitive Olympian, my insecurities that I wasn't sexy enough, combined with the thought that I was the only girl in the world who had been wanking all of these years – which I still genuinely thought – meant that, for me, sex and shame were intertwined.

I'm sure you've felt similar feelings of shame too? Maybe about how you look during sex. Or how many people you want to shag, or if you don't want to shag at all. You might be ashamed of the things that other people have done to you. And, beyond sex, you might have other sorts of shame.

Shame about how you cope with rejection. Shame about the horrible thoughts you have. Shame because you lied to your mum one time that you needed money to go for a pizza with your friends and you just spent it on cigarettes, chain-smoked them all, then lied to her about how good your margherita with doughballs was.

And you know what? We all deserve better than that. Well, most of you – some of you are probably beyond recovery (*cough* middle-aged man from Eton reading this book to try to understand the daughter he's failed to emotionally connect with). But the rest of you, reading this book, whoever you are, let me start by telling you one thing:

You deserve better than to feel ashamed of something that is completely normal.

This book is about all the shame we hold onto that doesn't belong in us. By letting you in on a lot of the shame I had, I hope you'll be able to let the shame you've experienced go. It might be similar to mine; it might be totally different. Whatever it is, it's all bullshit.

So, this is the deal: in reading this book, you will get to know a lot about me and my life. You'll get to know the good, the grim and the gorgeous. Lucky you. Some parts of my life have been pretty random. At the start I talk about politics, and after that privilege, as they were the things in my childhood that made me feel very lucky and sometimes very confused and scared. Chances are you probably didn't grow up in that kind of environment, but I'm pretty sure there were things in your childhood that had an impact on how you dealt with things as you got older. I know, I should be, like, Dr Phil or something.

You may have also noticed that on the cover of this book is an image of me on a dick-shaped cloud. Or a cloud-shaped dick? What do you think it is? I've already had multiple arguments with people about this. There are a lot of dicks in this book. Dick pics, dick owners and so many dickheads.

There is also a lot of rejection. Some traumatic sexual experiences (with a trigger warning included), some substance abuse, some self-loathing and a whole lot of jealousy.

But this is also a happy book. What with all of these twats who're running things right now, I don't want to bring more gloom into your life. Plus, I am generally a very happy person. Some say my smile can light up a million rooms. It was actually me that said that, but I think it's true. I light up my own room, that's for sure.

This book isn't just about shame. It's about female friendships, it's about love, it's about family and it's about incredible fucking sex. Because the truth is, I'm not at all ashamed of my vagina any more. In my bedroom I have a pot that was sculpted in the image of my vagina – that's how obsessed with my vagina I am.

So, you can expect a lot from me, because, as my parents say, I am 'a lot'. But this isn't a normal memoir, a step-by-step journey through my life. I'm too young to write one of those, for a start, plus I don't feel like it. I don't cover everything and there are some things I don't talk about at all. Some stories are short, and some are long, a bit like my relationships. You'll find some scripts along the way of how I wish conversations had gone, and some cute lists – lists that I've made to try to organise my shame. There's the occasional lesson, too. There aren't many, don't worry; I hate preaching, and this isn't a self-help book. Who ever learnt anything from a self-help book?

But my first story, you can learn from. This is my most important piece of advice:

DON'T FUCK A GUY IF HE CHATS SHIT ABOUT YOUR DAD

Let me set the scene. Because I want you to know who I was when I made this ill-fated sexual decision. I don't want you to read the title of this chapter and think, 'Who is this girl, bankrupt of morality? How can this sprightly young thing who's obsessed with herself make such a terrible miscalculation?' You need context.

I grew up in North-west London. This is, if you don't already know, the best part of London. I should add that everyone from North London is also very arrogant.

We lived right next to Hampstead Heath, which is a countryside utopia in the centre of London. Hampstead Heath would be offended if you called it a park; it's so much more than a park. It has ponds. Notice the plural there? We have multiple ponds that you can swim in. I was born in a hospital looking out over the heath, I grew up right next to it, and my secondary school, the comprehensive Parliament Hill School for Girls, backed out onto it. Hampstead Heath was where I became the glamorous gladiator that I now am.

And, sorry to brag again, but the best thing about Hampstead Heath were my friends. You'll meet them in a minute, but all you really need to know is that they made me feel safe. They made me feel like I had a normal upbringing.

This was important to me because, whatever I insist, there was something very abnormal about my upbringing. Throughout my childhood my dad, Alastair Campbell, had become someone of huge interest to the country because of his work with Tony Blair and the Labour Party, and also because of his general character. At the height of his power and fame, there were a lot of people who hated him. There were people who wanted him dead. We've got a long time to hang out together in this book, so I'll venture into the politics of my childhood later on. But right now, I just want to say this to you: when you are a child, politics means nothing to you. The Prime Minister could be in your house, sitting at your kitchen table, eating your Bourbon biscuits, flashing his massive teeth, and you just think he's another man in a suit who's turned up uninvited, without snacks, to interrupt your *Rugrats* viewing and talk about the polling.

All that mattered to me when I was younger was that I felt safe in my surroundings. And while my parents did so much to make me feel safe and loved, sometimes the situation we were in was unsettling. I didn't know how to deal with a lot of that when I was young. I mean, how can you when you're still watching *Hannah Montana*?

That's why I was obsessed with my friendship group. I was incredibly lucky to have that bubble when I did, because it meant I could grow up relatively oblivious to what *other* people thought about my dad. Obviously, I knew there were people who weren't his fans, but my friendship group made me feel so normal, and so secure, that I never really felt the intense impact of that.

Of course, that couldn't last forever, and when I finished school my bubble half burst. Those who could afford it, and had parents who could support them in doing so, took a gap yah and went to Thailand, Brazil or Cambodia. I went to Jamaica, because I'm original and I love reggae.

Then, after our gap yahs, most of the people I knew went to the same three universities: Sussex, Manchester or Leeds. I moved to Paris to study French at university. *Je parle français*, no need to make a big deal out of it. Please, stop. Fuck, I'm so shy. *Oui, j'adore français*.

I was at university in Paris for three months and I missed my friends desperately. I'd gone away without them on my gap yah but being in the Caribbean alone was fun, and people there were friendly and made me feel safe. Being in Paris without my friends made me feel unprotected.

In fact, I can't wait – let me give you a quick run-through of who they are right now:

There's Tyler, who I've known since I was very small. Tyler's really pretty but also with an edge, like Dolly Parton. I don't think anyone who has met Tyler dislikes her. She's the nicest person, but has always had the best instincts about people, and I basically take her judgements of people as the bible. Tyler didn't go to my secondary school (which I was fuming about), but throughout school she was still a permanent fixture in my life.

There's Anna, my beautiful and mouthy half-Greek, half-German school friend. Anna's loved by everyone, apart from the people that she dislikes. Anna will literally fight to defend my honour. In fact, just a few months before we all dispersed for uni, Anna physically fought a guy who had called me a slag at a party.

Then there's Emily, who I've known since before I was born. Our mums were best friends at school and we've lived on parallel roads our whole lives. Emily looks like she lives in LA, she knows everything about everything and she's NEVER tried alcohol or drugs in her life. You might think this is normal – perhaps you're one of my Amish fans – but in my friendship group, Emily was a mystery.

Next there's Jack. Jack is not built to be around sensitive people. He is incredibly honest and authentic and has the power to assassinate your character before you've even sat down to dinner, not because he wants to, but because he speaks his mind and is incapable of not doing so. Jack came out when we were eighteen. He has always been fiercely loyal, loving and the person that everyone wants to talk to at a party.

And then there's Leo. My very handsome straight best friend who is effortlessly cool and fancied by many. Leo and I were friends throughout school, and after we finished school he became very valuable in my safety bubble.

Anyway, sorry, I got a little distracted there, boasting about my gorgeous friends. Back to the story. When I got to Paris, I got crippling anxiety. Panic attacks so bad I felt I'd been drugged 24/7. The first one happened on the metro and lasted 5 hours and the whole time I was convinced if I left the underground world of the metro I would die. After that I became terrified of things like roofs falling in on me when I was inside a building, or the sky falling down when I was outside. Nowhere was safe for me. I found a therapist on Craigslist (big mistake) who I went to see and she convinced me that I was having a nervous breakdown, which made my mental state worse. My mum came to see me, and we worked out that I had anxiety. I went on medication, and I started to stabilise.

But really, what I needed in this time, was my friends. I was in no way ready to deal with life without them. And because I am lucky enough to have parents who could afford for me to come back, I did. It wasn't an easy decision – I felt like a failure – but I was anxious and miserable and we all knew where I needed to be. Hint: it begins with NW. Leo came to Paris, helped me pack up all of my things and brought me back home. Paris one. Grace nil.

As I've mentioned, when I began to have sex, aged eighteen, it wasn't quite what I'd hoped it'd be. By the time I got back from Paris, I was massively disappointed – let down even – by the sex I'd had so far. I was angry; so angry that I wanted to talk to the Manager of Sex. It didn't stop me doing it, it was just that I was doing it like it was another language I needed to become fluent in. Maybe as a replacement for French, *je ne sais pas*. I wondered if, the more I did it, the sooner the secret meaning would appear and sex would make sense. I just had to practise. But this is a tragic and futile investigation when you're having sex with boys whose entire understanding of sex comes from Pornhub.

They go from telling you at school that they lost their virginity to 'someone on a family holiday', which is an utter lie, to telling you they 'want to make you cum' when I'm pretty sure they don't even know the clit from the belly button. They think achieving the female orgasm is as easy as unlocking an iPhone; you just press your finger down long enough and voila! She'll squirt. (By the way, I am referring to the iPhone 7, not the ones with face ID. Although sometimes I do think men would like to just show their face to a clit and make it come . . . but then, that would require them to actually look at a vagina, with its hair and its skin, and . . . I'm not convinced all of them want to do that.)

Looking back, I realise I was too terrified to take control. I thought I was a freak who had been illegally humping things for years, and that if I let on that I knew how to make myself come, they'd tell everyone how much of a disgrace I was. Worse still, despite the fact that sex didn't give me the euphoric feeling that wanking did, I was already hooked on male validation. Ugh. The touch of a man. It was like eating a Twix and taking a fat line of cocaine at once. Feeling wanted by a man gave me a purpose. But just like cocaine, I got my quick fix and then the moment would pass, and I would be left feeling anxious and alone.

There were so many bad lovers. So many unsatisfying shags. The most unsatisfying of all was a man I met in Brighton. Let's call him 'unnamed man'. Not because I want to conceal his identity, I just can't remember his name. In my list of people I've shagged, he is down as 'Twat in Brighton'.

Not long after my dejected return from Paris, my friend Harriet had a fancy-dress party in Sussex. A reunion of the North-London massive. Surely that would cure my anxiety and restore my joy? This was clearly wildly delusional, though I was definitely very happy to be back on the soil that I've been pissing on my whole life.

Me, Emily, Jack and Leo drove down to Brighton in Emily's tiny, rickety car – a red Toyota we called Cherry, because Emily had lost her virginity in it. Emily was, of course, our designated driver, thanks to her early commitment to sobriety. We started drinking in the car, and even though it was still daylight when we got there, Jack, Leo and I were walking around Brighton like it was four in the morning and we were at a rave. We got to the party around midnight.

I had dressed up as a nun, so naturally all I wanted to do was have sex. I was like Julie Andrews's double in the porn version of *The Sound of Music*. *The Pound of Music*.

I got to the party and floated around, as nuns do. Across the dance floor I caught eyes with a guy who looked like he thought he was too cool to dance and so was standing bopping his head. He was good-looking in a basic white boy kind of way. He was tall and had good skin, which was a real currency then, when most people were going through post-pubescent skin breakouts. He looked like he loved football and hanging out with the lads. He looked at me across the dance floor.

Five minutes later, unnamed man and I were on our way out. It was like an Amazon Prime dick delivery. I ordered a dick, I blinked and the dick was there, albeit in a shit vampire costume. On the way out I signalled to Jack to tell him that I was leaving but promised I would be back.

Unnamed man and I got out into the street and were suddenly surrounded by silence. We started walking to his place, but making conversation felt like manual labour. I don't think he wanted to know anything about me. He was barely looking at me. I worried that he was regretting this spontaneous decision, now that he was out in the painful silence with me. Did I look different in the streetlights? Did he want to go back to the party? Maybe *I* wanted to go back to the party. I had a sudden longing for my friends who were back there. I missed the drugs and the spiced rum that I'd spent £10.99 on. Then I started worrying that my friends would forget about me, now that I'd left them for this . . . I didn't even know his name.

He got a cigarette out, which distracted me.

'Can I have one?'

'I'll share this one with you.'

'You have a whole packet of cigarettes. I'll have my own one, please.' He disliked me, I could tell. But he wasn't turning back.

'So . . . who did you vote for in the General Election last year?' I asked, because that is how I flirt. He was not finding it sexy.

'That's a weird question.' This conversation was clearly off to a banging start.

'Oh, okay . . . so you're a Tory?'

'No, I'm not a Tory.'

'So why won't you tell me who you voted for? I won't fuck you if you're a Tory.' I was 98 per cent bullshitting here. I probably would still have hate-fucked him if he was a Tory. I wouldn't have enjoyed it, but I would have made a thing out of it. I would have an anecdote about fucking a Tory that I could live off for many years to come. My kids would grow used to hearing about 'that one time that Mummy fucked a Tory'.

'Are you a Tory?' he asked.

'Tell me who you voted for first.' I wanted to be persistent, to show him I was dominant.

'I voted Green.'

'Oh, of course you did. Fuck, I'm so silly. You're a student living in Brighton!'

'Are you, like, a politician or something?' Here I was, in the presence of a genius. I started laughing uncontrollably. He didn't like that.

'Sure,' I said, 'I'm a politician that you just met at a student party! I crashed the party to focus-group the youth, find out what you are all interested in.' He didn't laugh with me. 'I'm Benjamin Button!' Still nothing. 'Of course I'm not a fucking politician,' I gestured to my giant black dilated pupils. I waited for him to react. An 'mmm' would have been nice.

What the fuck does this guy want from me? Does he want me to stop talking? Is he offended? Have I embarrassed him? If he *is* embarrassed, then maybe he deserves to be. It was a stupid question. No, I am being silly. This is really weird. He's weird, right? Or am I weird?

'My dad is Alastair Campbell . . .' I finally broke the silence with something I knew he couldn't ignore.

'Your dad's Alastair Campbell?!' unnamed man said. Fuck, he's a fan. This is going to be awkward.

'Your dad's a fucking wasteman!' He threw his cigarette into the road.

'Wasteman', if you don't know, is a word that originates from Jamaican patois. It is used to describe men who are a waste of space and haven't done much with their lives.

It has also been appropriated by middle-class white boys, and apparently they were now using it to describe my dad. This loser was calling my dad a wasteman? I stopped walking. I presumed this meant our Amazon dick-livery would be cancelled. But he carried on. 'I'm sure he'd feel the same about you!' I shouted.

'I'm sure he would, I'm about to fuck his daughter.'

•

I wish this story ended with me spitting on this twat's fresh pair of Converse, telling him to go fuck himself instead and turning around to go back to the party. I wish I'd known that this man wasn't going to make me feel safe. My friends back at the party would have made me feel safe. The friends who knew how much anxiety I had around who my dad is and what people think about him. I should have gone back to them. Especially because they had the rum.

But I didn't. I carried on, back to the unnamed man's house. A shithole of a house with ketchup sprayed all over the kitchen floor. I asked him for a glass of water and he said he didn't have cups. He filled a giant square Tupperware with water and passed it to me.

'Do you expect me to drink this like a fucking dog?'

'Sorry, we haven't bought cups yet.' I realised this is how people in student houses were living, and I vowed to myself that I would never live in such an unglamorous Tupperware lifestyle. He led me up to his room which was a concrete box with a bed in it that had probably survived both world wars. We started doing what we'd come here to do, but I was so detached from the situation I was like Moaning Myrtle, floating on the ceiling, watching this less-than-average sex play out.

My vagina was as dry as his conversation on our walk had been, but he still just stuck it in, because I don't think nineteen-year-old boys know about foreplay, lubricant, even just a bit of spit would have helped. His dick was like a mini-baguette that hadn't quite risen. He became frustrated that he couldn't get hard. I tried to kiss him and he refused. The sex ended unsatisfyingly. I knew it would also probably give me thrush. He brought me back to the party. I walked in and left him without looking back. I found Jack and Emily, who were sitting at the back of the garden with a group of boys we went to school with. Jack fixed my hair. 'What happened?' asked Emily.

'Yeah, we tried to fuck. It didn't happen. Also, he called my dad a wasteman.'

'What?? He slagged off Alastair? You should have bit his stinky dick off,' Jack said.

He was right.

•

The morning after that night in Brighton I felt like pure shit. I felt guilty for so many things. Guilty that I'd ditched my friends to have sex with someone who was rude about my dad. Guilty that I'd left the people who care about me the most for some quick fix from someone who cared more about his Tupperware cup than me.

Mostly I was ashamed that I didn't back myself more, that I didn't know this wasn't acceptable. But the truth is, I was in a bad place and I didn't rate myself enough to say no to just a bit of attention. That's what happens when we don't rate ourselves highly – we self-destruct. You've done that, too, right? For my sanity, I hope your answer is yes.

What I can see, looking back on that night, is that I was avoiding confronting a lot of things about myself. Firstly, who my dad was, and what impact that had on my child-hood and mental health. Then there was my drinking and drug-taking, and why I always seemed compelled to take things to an extreme level in the hope that it would distract me from the impending doom of loneliness in my head. And finally, the fact that I used men as a distraction to really acknowledge how I felt about myself.

I hope that story doesn't put you off me. I care a lot about what people think of me, you know? That might surprise you if you've ever met me, because I am good at giving off the vibe that I don't care what people think of me. I try really hard to give the impression that I don't give a shit. But I do. Maybe you can relate to that, too.

Either way, if that story made you like me or not, I want to thank you for picking up this book, it means so much to me. I hope you stay with me, in my world, for this book. I love you and I hope you love me, too.

WHY MY PARENTS WILL NEVER DIE

So, **Tony Blair** stole the thunder of my birth. Very unrelatable, I know – I promise it gets more relatable soon. But it's true. When I was born I was like, 'Hello, everyone, *je suis arrivée*. Time for you all to shut the fuck up and *écoutez-moi* (listen to me)!' And for the first few weeks of my life I did have my parents' attention. They were obsessed with this red-faced Cabbage Patch doll they'd created.

Then, when John Smith, then leader of the Labour Party, suddenly died, Tony Blair decided to run to be the new party leader, and there was only one man he wanted to run his campaign. The same man I wanted to change my nappies. My dad.

My parents had become friends with Tony in the early Nineties, when both of them were journalists. My parents actually met doing a journalism trainee scheme in Devon, and they moved in with each other a week after meeting. True love, I always say, but my mum says my dad fell in love with her mainly because she had a nice car. When they met Tony, they were proper journalists on Fleet Street. Power coupling of course. Tony Blair was meanwhile an up-and-coming Member of Parliament. I imagine they'd crossed paths with him at boring political functions in Westminster. Functions that always had cheap wine and terrible canapés.

Now that Tony was tipped to become the next leader of the Labour Party, he wanted my dad to ditch his career and family to come and work for him and help promote their idea of 'New Labour', a venture which I was sure had been inspired by my mum's birth of me.

My dad was reluctant at first because he didn't want to leave us. But Tony persisted – he stank of desperation, to be honest. He even turned up on my first holiday, in France, which is creepy as fuck, and spent the whole time trying to persuade my dad to work for him. He had this weird toothy smile which was the inspiration for my first ever nightmare.

But Tony won this campaign, as he was about to win many more, and after much persuasion my dad agreed to take on the job, and here lay my first experience of rejection, because then my dad was gone. Not completely, but a lot more than I wanted him to be. He had a fair reason, sure, he was running a political campaign. Did I care for his excuse? No. I felt abandoned. My parents were off 'on the campaign trail', which I'd hoped was a game they'd let me play, but they never did.

The next time I was upstaged by Tony Blair was on my third birthday. Everyone knows your third birthday is as important as your eighteenth or your fiftieth. And Tony wanted to ruin this for me, too. That was the day that Tony chose to become Prime Minister for the first time. I'm sure he picked that day just so he could piss on my parade once more.

In the BBC footage of that monumental moment, I am there, outside Downing Street, in my mum's arms, directly next to Tony Blair, who is making a typical politician's speech about how 'you can put your faith in me', and 'I will transform this country', blah. And you can see very clearly that I would rather be at home talking gibberish to my Furbies, who I was busy training to attack Tony Blair.

After my third birthday, I was sick of hearing about Tony Blair, and I thought I wouldn't have to any more. I thought that now Tony Blair had won and he'd moved into his new house on Downing Street, that surely my dad's job was done?

How naive I was, little three-year-old me. How could I be so stupid? After Tony got into power, both of my parents started working full-time for him at Downing Street. My dad was Tony Blair's head of communications, and my mum, Fiona, was a special advisor to Tony's wife, Cherie. I thought Cherie was French, because of course by then I was mildly bilingual from the holiday we'd been on, but unfortunately she wasn't. Another let-down.

And there began the most dominant force of my childhood: my parents' careers. My brilliant parents were now splitting their attention between me and politics. I mean, what the fuck? I was so much cuter than politics. But now politics was the other member of our family, and I didn't understand why. I was born, and straight away my life got weird. My parents' careers would get me into powerful places, but they would also royally fuck me up.

•

My parents have always been attractive. I'm not super shallow or anything, but I think about how good-looking they are one to fifteen times a day. Seriously, my mum has looked exactly the same for as long as I've known her. Twenty-six years of being *my* mum and she's not aged. I thought being the mother of an attention-seeking, bulldozer hypochondriac would have aged her like smoking does. But no, she's the spitting image of Kirsten Cohen from *The* OC. But unlike Kirsten Cohen, my mum's never had plastic surgery. Her face is untouched by a needle.

How does she do it?! Well, she's the epitome of health. She swims more than some fishes do; she's swum every day of her life since she was nineteen years old. She's a vegetarian – doesn't even eat fish because she basically is one. She barely drinks alcohol, and when she does, after one glass of rosé she'll say, 'Oh, I've got to stop now, if I drink any more I'll get a headache.'

Meanwhile, I drink rosé like it's water and have a headache if I've drunk less than two glasses of it. I will never achieve my mum's level of commitment to health, and I'll be honest, it did used to fuck me up that by fourteen I was bigger, wider and less buff than my mum. Going shopping together was a nightmare because whenever I'd put something on that didn't fit, I'd somehow manage to blame her for the fact that a size 8 pair of Topshop jeans were too small for me. Now, in my twenties, I've learnt to be proud of how dedicated to health she is, and I bask in the reflected glory of her gorgeousness.

My dad's pretty gorgeous, too. He was once voted Hunk of the Year by the *Gay Times* when the year before it had been David Beckham! Women really fancied my dad when I was younger, but my mum has never cared because, well, she's buffer than Dad anyway.

As a child, I can't remember ever being embarrassed by my parents. I always really enjoyed hanging out with them, when they were there. But they weren't always there. This isn't a sob story, by the way; I know it's very normal for kids to have parents who have jobs. All I'm saying is that absence certainly made my heart grow fonder. When I had them there, I was like one of those puppies who gets so overexcited about the fact that their owners are at home that they get tail-wagging strain. When they weren't there, I didn't think a huge amount about what they were doing. I couldn't have cared less about their jobs. All I cared about was that they were there to watch my performances; whether it be Britney Spears inspired dances, or my interpretation of the musical *Annie*.

Like many parents, my mum and dad would go off to work every day. My mum would get up at 5.30 a.m. to go for a swim, then she'd come back and my dad would leave before 7 a.m. He'd jog down to Westminster in shabby exercise clothes he's had since the Eighties – my dad doesn't believe in buying new clothes, very thrifty like that. And my mum would go later, once we'd all gone to school. Their job was not nine to five. Politics is an addictive, all-consuming world with an ongoing stream of drama. When you're working in the thick of it, you can't sleep, you can't relax and you definitely can't come. That is why I was my parents' last child. This is an assumption I'm sure they won't mind me voicing.

My two older brothers, Rory and Calum, are seven and six years older than me. This means they had a long period of what I call PTT; 'Pre-Tony Time'. They have a different relationship with my parents as a result of this; they weren't as obsessed with getting attention because they'd already had quite a lot of it.

I am SO different to both of my brothers. It was as if we came out of the same vagina, but they came through the normal entrance into the audience and I took the wrong door and came out on the stage. They were quieter, whether through confidence or independence, and they had each other. And they had football. My brothers were such boys. They would have swapped me for a Nintendo and a Burnley season ticket if they could have. I don't think they thought they could get much out of a sister. But I was so desperate to impress them that my first words were 'Gary Neville'. I'm not joking. 'Gary Neddle' was more how I said it, but those were my first words, in a huge effort to get my brothers to endorse me.

But they never did, not in the way they endorsed other boys. I'd never be cool enough for them because I wasn't a boy. And at the same time I also felt I'd never be cool enough for my parents because I wasn't Tony Blair. They were off doing Tony Blair things. My dad especially was off on private planes. He was meeting Nelson Mandela. He was talking to the Spice Girls, and how could I compete with that?

I didn't feel that there was anyone in my life who was on my level.

Then one day, when I was eight years old, my mum and I were walking home from Marks & Spencers. I'd bought some of those chocolate cornflake bars that really put M&S on the map back then. I was gobbling down the cornflake bars, forgetting to chew them and choking, which is a permanent eating state for me. My mum was telling me to save some room for dinner, as if there had ever been an occasion when I hadn't saved enough space for dinner.

At the top of my road, we bumped into my mum's friend, Kim, who was with her daughter Tyler. Kim and my mum started to catch up, and Tyler and I lingered behind. We started talking about Mary-Kate and Ashley Olsen, who I was obsessed with. 'I have all of their films on VHS,' Tyler said, not bragging.

'Why doesn't Grace come over and they can hang out?' Kim said to my mum. The next day I went over to

Tyler's after school. We watched *Passport to Paris*. We enacted scenes from the film. We played out my fantasy of what having a sister was like. Tyler was an only child, who was also looking for a sister. Tyler and I became one person.

Tyler never minded that I was the bossiest kid in the world. I never minded that everyone thought she was sweeter than I was, because it was undeniably true. Tyler never stressed about the fact that I had a tendency of getting into fights with other kids in the neighborhood if they said something mildly rude to me. I didn't mind that Tyler always knew how to defuse the situation. She's never been stubborn and didn't care that I am a Taurean bulldog. Tyler and I were the non-identical, North-London, ruder versions of Mary-Kate and Ashley.

I thank the Olsen twins every day that they brought me Tyler when they did. Because over the course of our childhoods, things got pretty messy. Messy like an England fan at a World Cup. But having Tyler was like always having a constant deep breath. Even when things got crazy, it seemed completely normal, because Tyler was there.

I didn't expect things to get weird and unstable. I was a bang average child. I didn't have super powers like Matilda. I was just a girl who loved shopping at the Gap and knocking on my neighbours' doors and then running away. I was a girl who was totally obsessed with her parents. Mildly interested in her brothers. Borderline in love with her best friend. I was too young and preoccupied with the inner workings of my little world to take much interest in what my parents actually did. Perhaps if I had, I might have predicted that very soon the outside world was going to come into my house with no warning and shake things up like a bad case of asbestos.

•

When I was nine I looked seven, and in my head I was a mature twenty-five-year-old. And in my ninth year, my life became even more dramatic than a Mary-Kate and Ashley movie. I was becoming a bit more trouble. I think as I was growing older I was getting more of a sense of my parents' lives outside our house. I both wanted them with me and wanted to be with them, wherever they went. I was starting to see how much of a profile my dad had. And so what I wanted to do was redirect that attention back onto me.

At school, I was getting into fights. On my road, I was getting into fights. I even got kicked out of my running club, the Highgate Harriers, for my incessant use of the word 'fuck'. At the time my dad was getting a reputation for being a shouty, sweary spin doctor, and clearly, I was acting out in the only way I knew how: by acting like him.

My mum started working from home more. I loved this because I could finally perform my interpretation of the musical *Annie* for her. But there was still a tension, and I'm sure like a dog smelling a tsunami before the humans can, I could feel something was coming.

It came on a Friday morning. What I heard first sounded like chanting. I thought it was coming from the radio in the kitchen downstairs, but when I moved closer to the front of the house, I could hear it was people shouting outside. When I looked out of the window I saw a huge group of scruffy-looking adults wearing oversized T-shirts with my dad's face on. Were they . . . mega-fans? I looked at their placards, which also had my dad's face on them, but now he had blood coming out of his mouth and he was wearing devil horns. The words 'Alastair Campbell = War Criminal' flashed up over and over again. Probably not mega-fans then. But surely my dad wasn't a criminal? I knew he swore a lot, but I didn't think that was actually a crime. In fact, I thought he was an angel.

The adults in T-shirts made me feel weird. They were chanting slogans about my dad, and I could hear the unrestrained anger in their voices. I didn't understand exactly why they were there, but I knew they were trying to attack my family and I took this very personally. Anyone who has beef with my dad has beef with me. And I'm the only one allowed to slag him of. All right? Don't @ me.

I needed to show them I was a tough little firecracker who wouldn't be scared by their unrhythmical chants.

Even if I was shaking in my *101 Dalmatians* pyjamas, they couldn't know it. I decided to bring the scrappy kid who got into fights at school to the crowd of intimidating adults outside her front door.

I put on a pair of skorts. Do you remember them? They were the skirt/short hybrid that little girls wore strictly in 2003. I knew nothing would scare a group of old protesters more than a skort. I wore them with a blue T-shirt with a parrot and the words 'Listen to me' on it. I gave myself a nod in the mirror. A supportive nod, like Lady Gaga walking past her warm-up act before a show at Madison Square Gardens. I went down the flight of stairs facing the front door, and as I did I could hear the crowd; it sounded louder than it had before. In that moment I learnt how to seem okay when I was far from it. A useful skill, might I add, although one with long-lasting side effects.

In the kitchen, my mum was listening to Radio 4, as ever.

'Mum, who are those people outside?' I asked, pouring a hefty amount of Coco Pops into my bowl. It's important to eat before a major battle with badly dressed adults.

'Oh, darling,' my mum said. 'They're here because they've got a . . . problem with Dad.' She looked at me for a long moment and then walked to the radio and turned it off.

'Why are they here, though?'

'Because of the war,' she said, as if that would tie up all of the loose ends flying around in my head. Because of the war?

'Are they going to attack Dad?'

'No, no, darling, they'll just shout when they see him. They're not going to hurt you, or any of us, okay?'

'Okay.' I carried on eating. I wondered if she was scared . . . she didn't look scared.

'Is Dad going to be okay at work?'

'He's going to be fine. He's very safe. They're not going to hurt any of us, okay?' I was doubtful of this; their T-shirts were so badly designed I already felt visually violated by their pathetic Photoshop skills.

My mum passed me a few bottles of Volvic water. 'Will you give them these on the way out?'

'To the people outside . . .?'

'Yes, they'll get thirsty.'

This confused me, but also made me feel like they probably weren't going to kill us. I opened the door to them. Their faces were wearing a lot of rage, though they calmed down a bit when they saw how young I was. They watched me walk out like I was a cabaret act at a funeral. I felt deeply uncomfortable.

After assessing them as a group, I decided that the woman with the megaphone and visor was the unofficial leader. She was the one leading the chants. Maybe in another life we would have been kindred spirits, but right now she was a threat to me.

'My mum wants to give you this water, if you get thirsty.'

Megaphone lady didn't say anything. I put the water down on our garden wall, right next to a huge Tupperware box filled with tuna sandwiches and boiled eggs. This made me feel weird – that these protestors had woken up extra early and made a packed lunch so they could come and protest outside my house. It made me think they couldn't be evil, but that their farts probably stank, and perhaps that was part of their battle, bringing an egg 'n' cress stink to my street as a form of protest against my dad. Creatively done.

Obviously I told everyone at school about the protestors as if it was a bit I was doing on stage. And by the end of the day I'd built it into a mad adventure. By that evening Tyler and I were sitting at the upstairs window watching the protestors and I'd forgotten any sense of feeling unsafe. By this time the sandwiches were eaten, the water had been drunk and the protestors looked bored.

'I know, let's stick our tongues out at them,' I said.

'Okay, one, two, three . . .' We stuck our tongues out aggressively, shaking them around so that they eventually noticed us. They looked up, and we kept sticking our tongues out generously, pressing our faces up against the windows. They looked bemused. Tyler and I found this hilarious. But then our childish assault against a group of weary protestors was interrupted by the arrival of two police officers.

'Oh, the police are here!' Tyler said.

'They're probably going to arrest the protestors!' I shouted. We were finally living in a movie.

We ran downstairs; the two male police officers were now sitting comfortably at our kitchen table. They weren't here to arrest the protestors; they wanted to talk to us. Fuck. We're being arrested for sticking our tongues out at them.

Of the two officers, I found the visibly older one very off-putting. He was more assertive and whenever he spoke the room stank of his cigarette breath. I noticed he had a hole in his ear from when he'd once had it pierced.

The other one was cute and reminded me of Duncan from Blue, the band I was utterly obsessed with at the time. My mum made the officers a cup of tea while my brothers, Tyler and I sat around the kitchen table. DC Cigarette Breath started talking about the 'new protocol' that my family were going to have now that we were an 'at risk' household. Tyler and I were squeezing each other's hands under the table.

'We'll be checking up on your house every hour in an undercover car, just to check there's no unusual events happening outside,' he started. I didn't understand what he meant by this.

'Surely, if you were in a police car that would be more scary to people?' Rory asked him. Good question, Rory, I wish I'd asked that. DC Cigarette Breath looked at Rory, who was a genius teenager by now, and then carried on talking.

'And then there are the panic buttons,' he said. He looked at me directly and said, 'Kid, the panic buttons are only to be pushed if you're in real danger, okay?'

The younger officer pitched in, finally. He has a voice! 'If you're in danger, you stick your fingers right into the buttons and someone from our team will be here within seconds.' His voice was gorgeous. Put that soundbite straight into the wank bank.

'Yeah, Grace, not when you want me to get you an ice lolly from the shop, okay?' my mum said. I didn't appreciate her talking to me like a child in front of Duncan.

I didn't want to ask how I would know if I was in danger. It felt like we were already in danger, and anyway, I knew they'd lie to me. After the police left, Tyler had to go home for dinner, so I sat on my bedroom floor, staring into the eyes of the panic buttons. They weren't really buttons, but two square holes you had to stick your fingers into. I was eyeing them up, flirting with their little plastic pockets, thinking about the way DC Duncan from Blue described sticking my fingers in them.

I needed to know how quickly the police would really come if I stuck my fingers in there. Would it be seconds? Or were they just showing off? What if there was traffic, or one of them had the shits? They should have let us have a test run with them. How else could I trust they would actually work?

I got so close to sticking my fingers into those tiny buttons I honestly think they're the reason I got so avidly into fingering. Fingering was a distraction from fingering the buttons on the wall. Fingering was an alternative, for me, to getting into trouble with the police. Instead of fingering the panic buttons, I fingered myself ... I had graduated from humping Toby the Tory. I was a fingerer now.

But what happened that day wasn't about fingering. It was about war. That's much bigger than fingering. Feel free to quote me on that.

The protestors came to stand outside my house that day and every day for months afterwards because they wanted to protest against the UK's decision to invade Iraq. Now that I'm an adult I can see that the protestors had a point, though they should have gone to Tony's house, not mine. I think the Iraq War was an awful, unnecessary tragedy that didn't need to happen – 470,000 people lost their lives directly or indirectly from the Iraq War. It broke up entire communities, and we're still seeing the consequences of it today.

If, on that Friday morning, I had been a twenty-one-year-old who read the *Guardian*, I would have gone outside and tried to reason with the megaphone lady. I would have told her I'm on her side. She would have offered me a boiled egg and reluctantly I would have eaten it, promising her that I would try to help.

But I was nine, and even if I had understood what was happening in Iraq, I don't think there's much I could have done. Should I have refused to eat my greens at dinner? Should I have said, 'Dad, I'm not eating my broccoli unless you promise me you will tell Tony he can't invade Iraq'? I didn't know what the fuck was going on around me, and selfishly the only campaign I wanted to fight at the time was *my* campaign to get a puppy.

The Iraq War brought a lot of friction into my house. Not sexy friction. Very un-sexy friction. My parents were at war about the war. The war was pushing them apart because they both had differing opinions. My mum was anti the war, and my dad obviously wasn't. Listening to their sizzling-hot fights, I thought they might break up. Tyler's parents had split up, and I knew that this was a reality that I should get ready for. My mum was obviously conflicted. She was angry that this job was now putting all of us in danger, and all for something she didn't agree with, but also, she wanted to protect my dad, because she loved him, in the same way I loved Duncan from Blue at the time.

The day those tuna-eating protestors came chanting about my dad outside our house, my life changed. Panic buttons make you panic, even if you don't have to press them. They're there because you might panic. And this made me panic.

I absorbed the tension without really knowing where it belonged. Tyler was my North Star. We just kept doing what we did. Mary-Kate and Ashley were replaced by Tony Hawk. We got obsessed with skateboarding, and Tyler's Aunt Liz bought us Red Hot Chili Peppers limited-edition skateboards. We became so dedicated to skateboarding that we spent eight months learning how to stand on it, and about a year later we could finally ride down the street. Our neighbours told us off for doing it on the pavement, so we did it in the road, then they slagged us off for doing it in the road, so I stuck my middle finger up at them and we carried on.

•

I've had fears of my parents dying since I could form thoughts in my head. But when the protestors turned up and the panic buttons arrived, my irrational fears turned into more legitimate ones.

I became obsessed with the idea of them dying. This wasn't a healthy kind of obsession. It could never lead anywhere good in my psyche. I'd play out scenarios in my head, imagining ways it might happen. Someone would shoot my dad when he'd be out with my mum, and they'd accidentally shoot my mum, too.

Needing to take this anxiety and turn it into a responsibility, I decided I had to get a job. I hired myself as my dad's bodyguard. I was the only one who could protect him. My first shift as his bodyguard was at the Royal

Festival Hall. My dad was doing a live show to a sold-out audience, presumably because he was carpe diem-ing the moment of still being pretty mega in the UK. You never know when it might end, so I respect this.

So we went to see my dad at the Festival Hall. The event went on quite late, past my usual bedtime, but I was working so I had an excuse for the next day. After the event my dad was mingling in the lobby of the venue and a very small, very circular woman approached him, wagging her finger. 'You've got nerve coming here and doing this!' she shouts at my dad. 'You're a criminal!' My dad laughed it off, knowing people were watching. But I started growling.

'You paid money to be here!' I shouted.

'No, I didn't, I got these tickets as a present!' And then she was gone.

This stuff happened a lot in those days. It was a strange feeling to realise that my hilarious and very loving dad had this external life that left him exposed. I looked up to him so much, but during this time I realised that not everyone thought he was so great.

Wherever we went circa 2003–05, he was a verbal punching bag for random people on the street who thought they were the first ones to confront him. They thought they were so original, heckling him at dinner. I would roll my eyes and be like, 'Hun, bit boring. Can you at least find something new to say?' He'd get heckled on trains. A train is the worst place to get heckled, because you can't get away from the hecklers. I would always make him sit in the window seat, with me in the aisle seat, so there was a barrier between him and the heckler. Basically, children are the best security for celebrities, because people are much less likely to properly kick off in front of a child. I now understand that this is why celebrities love showing off their children. You might be thinking, how did I handle this? Was I scared? The answer is, yes, I was terrified, but it was my job, and I've never been a quitter.

My job was to protect my dad, because he always had to pretend he was fine. You see, there were two versions of my dad. The version in the outside world where he had to be Alastair Campbell. A six-foot-three tough guy who laughs off abuse and couldn't give a shit what people thought about him. Then there was Big Al. Him at home, lying on the sofa with a bowl of Kettle Chips on his stomach, fast asleep.

Big Al started appearing a lot more after 2003, when my dad resigned from his job at Downing Street. Finally, I could show him my modern interpretation of *Annie*, the musical, too. But I didn't get to, because as soon as my dad quit Downing Street, he had a breakdown. He became depressed and anxious, and to be honest I thought he was turning into a bit of a vampire. He's had depression on and off for longer than I've been alive, but he'd been working in politics so intensely during my life that it had kept his mental-health issues at bay. But now, I was having the first of many encounters with my dad's depression.

It's no surprise that this happened right after he left his job. If you'd spent the last decade of your life stressing out about Tony Blair and New Labour, sometimes getting it right, sometimes getting it wrong, barely stopping to give yourself time to do a shit or see your family, you'd fall hard and fast into a ditch when you finished that job, too, I guarantee it.

It was a side of my dad I'd never seen before. I was used to him being the one who was in charge; like Alex Ferguson at Manchester United, my dad was the manager of our team. And now he was being overruled by something bigger than him. He would lie in bed all day with the curtains closed, in the dark, and I'll be honest, I took it very personally. Because I thought I'd done something wrong to make him feel this way. He was happy before when he was off in private jets with Tony, and now he was back with me he had this glazed look in his eyes – so I thought it must be something I'd done.

'Dad, let's go to the cinema!'

'I can't today, Gracie.' His voice was completely flat.

'*Cheaper by the Dozen* is out! We were meant to see it together.'

'We will. I promise. Tomorrow?'

'Okay.' I went to leave. 'Have I done something wrong?'

'No,' he said. He looked so sad. 'You've done nothing wrong.'

I had no idea that even me saying that made him feel so much worse, because he hated feeling like he was also making his kids feel bad. But honestly, as a self-absorbed nine-year-old, it was impossible not to take that personally.

The next day my dad managed to get out of bed and we went to the cinema. Finally, I had him to myself, and I felt this huge responsibility to make him feel better.

We did our usual cinema ritual: we liked to steal pick 'n' mix. Cue headlines saying 'ALASTAIR CAMPBELL IS A THIEF', but come on, guys, chill out, like, one chocolate raisin, for a laugh. Also, to the Vue Cinema in Finchley Road, when I'm mega-rich I promise I'll pay you back for all the stolen pick 'n' mix. (P.S. A great example of white privilege is being able to steal pick 'n' mix as a 'ritual' because you are sure you'll never get arrested.)

I was so excited to see *Cheaper by the Dozen* because, well, Hilary Duff was in it, for God's sake. If you haven't seen *Cheaper by the Dozen*, please stop reading this book and quickly go and watch it, I need you to understand the mastery of it. Basically, it's a film about a couple, played by Steve Martin and Bonnie Hunt, who have twelve children. The premise is that Steve Martin is a chaotic father who gets offered an amazing job coaching a huge football team, and he decides to uproot his family's life because of his career, and his twelve kids are fuming because they wanted to stay where they are. My dad and I loved this kind of film.

There's a scene at the end of the film when Steve Martin's character is surprised by his children on the pitch of the football team he coaches, which is their way of finally showing that they approve of his decision to move them all. Are you crying yet?

My dad was. He was sobbing in the boiling-hot Vue Cinema. I'd never heard him make such a sound in my life. Luckily the cinema was empty so no one could report that Alastair Campbell (war criminal and pick 'n' mix thief) was heard crying in the Vue Cinema in Finchley Road.

I didn't know what to do. Was I supposed to . . . cry with him? Would a joint cry make him feel better? Should I get him a tissue? I felt guilty for bringing him to see this film – I'd thought it would cheer him up. But here he was, crying. I had to help him somehow. I decided to do what the kids in the film were doing and gave him a squeeze. He squeezed me back. When we left the cinema, I could see he was lighter. He had the early remnants of a smile on his face, which I hadn't seen for a while. And for that, I thank myself.

And, I guess, Steve Martin.

•

While I was adjusting to my parents being back on the scene and my dad's depression being a new member of our family, Tyler was also dealing with a lot in her family. I'd known Tyler had a complicated family set-up since I'd met her. Her mum, Kim, lived nearby. Her aunt, Liz, lived on my road, three doors down. Her dad, Pete, had just recently moved to the road at the top of mine. Tyler moved between these three homes, but none of the three adults in Tyler's life spoke to each other. 'Why?' I once asked Tyler.

'I think because my mum drinks too much alcohol.'

Kim was always a great host when we'd go round there. She loved to spoil Tyler and me. But her drinking had been an ongoing problem in Tyler's life, and I had been too self-involved to realise how bad it had gotten.

Then my mum sat me down one day after Tyler had gone home. 'Tyler's mum's going away for a bit.'

'Where to?' I said.

'She's going to rehab,' my mum said, talking to me like the nine-year-old adult I was, which I appreciated. 'For her drinking.'

'What's wrong with her drinking?' I asked.

'She's just got an addiction to alcohol. It's an illness,' she said. 'Your dad used to have one, and he's fine now.' I mean, that's questionable, I thought, remembering how often he had been asleep on the sofa all day.

'Is Tyler going with her?' I panicked that we'd be separated and then we'd never get to go to Thorpe Park for her birthday.

'No, Tyler will stay here, she'll just live with her dad and Liz. She's going to really need you to be there for her, okay?'

'Tyler is my best friend. I'll be there for her.'

I felt guilty that while I'd been panicking about the panic buttons, Tyler had been panicking, too, and she didn't have any panic buttons to protect her and her mum.

If I was good at pretending I was okay with the external conditions of my life, Tyler did it like it was an art form. Tyler never admitted if she was struggling; she hated people knowing what was going on at home. So, because we were children who didn't have the language to talk about what was happening internally, we carried on doing what we knew how to do. We worried about bad things happening to our parents, we ignored the things actually happening to them and we started growing up.

THINGS TYLER AND I DID FOR THE FIRST TIME BETWEEN 2004 AND 2007

- Get drunk on WKD.

- Go to the Hard Rock Café alone and smoke a cigarette on the way home.

- Snog boys at an underage rave at ULU, the University of London's Union, and then get picked up by my mum at 7 p.m. with love bites on our necks.

- Talk about our emotions.

- Go to a proper house party with a pool, weed, and no parents.

- Go to Thorpe Park and get concussed on Colossus.

- Buy fake IDs online – our fake names were Summer and Marissa (*The OC*), but unfortunately we got the maths wrong and on our new fake IDs we were still underage.

●

When Tyler was fourteen years old, she got the news that she'd silently been dreading for a lot of her life. Kim had died. Tyler had lost her mum. Kim had been trying to get sober for Tyler. Kim loved her daughter so much that she'd wanted to be sober so badly.

But sadly alcoholism is an illness, and sometimes it becomes bigger than the person it's living in, and in this case it had harmed Kim's body so badly that even when she'd got sober, her liver was too far gone.

Kim's funeral was devastating. I don't think there was anyone there who wasn't crying – for Kim, but also for Tyler. When I was sat in the crematorium with my parents, I felt so guilty that Tyler, my guardian angel, was having to say goodbye to her mum when we were still children.

Originally, I wasn't going to talk about Kim in this book, because it's Tyler's story, not mine. But when I mentioned I was writing a lot about our childhoods Tyler said to me, 'I think you should write about my mum.'

'Are you sure?' I asked.

She said this:

I feel totally comfortable with you writing about my mum. I think it's so important talking about this type of grief. It's so hard, especially when you're young and don't quite know how to process it. That sometimes does take time. It did with me. And it's equally hard for friends and family to know how to support you. I think young people who have alcoholic parents feel like they're the only ones . . . I definitely did. And for that reason alone, you should definitely talk about it, because someone else might find comfort in this part of our story. It shouldn't be written out.

Lylas xxxxxx

I'm so grateful to Kim for giving me Tyler. It's funny that I thought I was my dad's guard dog, but I never realised how much Tyler was mine. Tyler has always been a constant. Tyler settled my whole family, even though she was feeling unsettled herself. Since Kim died I've learnt so much from Tyler, about how you deal with grieving a parent. And her bottom line is this: it's never easy, but you just have to survive it. I'm so proud of Tyler for surviving what happened to her. For being able to talk about it now. For trusting her friends to understand and for being able to ask for what she needs from other people. When we were younger we didn't talk about the things that we were really scared of, that were happening around us – but now Tyler and I have realised how that period affected us, and we can now articulate the trauma that it created. And we're both still wonderfully obsessed with each other.

I know now that a lot of my anxieties around death come from 2003, and 2003 alone. A lot happened for me in that year. As an adult, when I've done therapy, we always come back to those days when my body and mind were whacked into different time zones.

That period created this wild melting pot of anxiety and neuroses in my head, and so many of my fears were focused on my parents dying – frankly, they still are. Watching Tyler be so incredibly brave and strong has made me feel ashamed at the thought that I wouldn't be able to cope. Sometimes my mind still lets me spiral out of control with those old fears.

Just recently, I saw my dad's name trending on Twitter. Fuck. I put my oat-milk latte down, my chest clamped down. He's dead. He's had a heart attack. He's been shot by a woman with a megaphone and a boiled egg. Why else would he be trending?

I click on his name with a fearful, heavy heart. And what I see at the top of the thread is an article saying, 'Alastair Campbell kicked out of the Labour Party for anti-Brexit pro-Lib Dem vote in Euro elections'. Really, Dad? Was it worth it?

Every time I see my dad is trending on Twitter, that is my natural reaction. I go through the motions that he's died. I think about his funeral. I worry about how the media will move into our front garden again. And can you blame me? We're living in a world where one UK politician has been murdered and others face constant death threats, as my dad has been since I was a small child. So maybe it's simply my natural instinct as his daughter to fear the worst when I see he's trending.

I am aware that I am extremely lucky to have had both of my parents for as long as I have, and I am so grateful for that, but what I've realised as I've grown up is that fearing the loss of people you love is a part of life. There is no shame in being afraid of death – it's actually one of my more rational fears. I always say that the only guarantees in this world are death and thrush. And as a great (still alive) man called Alastair Campbell always says to me, which is a quote he nicked from the Queen, 'Grief is the price we pay for Love.'

I sound so wise, don't I? Who is this incredibly mature, sophisticated woman who's not scared of anything? Maybe I don't need to rely on my parents at all. Maybe soon they'll start relying on me. Good luck to them if so. But for now, I am still as obsessed with them as ever. I still want to hang out with them all the time. I still want to crash dates that they go on. And I still call my mum forty times a day.

REASONS WHY I CALL MY MUM

- When I'm constipated.

- When I sneeze and think I have cancer.

- If my period is late.

- When I forget my jean size.

- Whenever I get a haircut.

- After I cook a vegetarian meal.

- When I need money.

- When I watch a good TV show with Reese Witherspoon in it.

- Whenever I've been rejected.

- If I'm walking somewhere.

- If she doesn't reply to my texts.

- When I crash my rental car and need her to call the insurance.

WHY AM I NOT THE PRIME MINISTER?

The 2000s were like a mix of sweet and salty popcorn for me. I remember going to see David Blaine (the magician) in a suspended glass box next to the Tower of London, where he was starving himself for forty-four days while people threw egg and cress sandwiches at him. I remember Britney Spears becoming Britney. I remember my dad getting Twitter in its first inception, when we all still had Nokia phones, and he would text his tweets out and they'd somehow appear on the worldwide web. I remember *Big Brother* and being allowed to watch it with my big brothers when my parents weren't there.

And, of course, I remember Tony Blair. Anthony Charles Lynton Blair. A severely pompous name, don't you think? For most of the Noughties, we were living in Blair's Britain, a fact that I couldn't avoid as a child. Obviously, the tyrant Tories being gone: fantastic. A party in power that cares about the vulnerable in society: incredible. But as you know, while Blair was in Number 10, I was a little preoccupied trying to figure out how some middle-aged man with a smile that looks like it catches a hundred flies a minute was more important than me.

I couldn't understand why Tony Blair was such a big deal, to be honest. My dad's office, at one point, looked out over Downing Street itself. I used to go and sit in the bay window, watching the police officers who were standing at either end of the street, and I would wonder to myself, 'What is so important about Tony Blair that he needs this much protection?'

I was surrounded by men who had power. Men who had secretaries, and bodyguards, and people who carried their bags and looked after their passports. At Downing Street, I picked up on the hype around men, and I wanted in.

I completely idolised my dad. I'd watch him go off every day to his powerful job, with his office, and his secretary, and his briefcase, which contained his giant notepad, and I wanted to be just like him. I wanted to wear a suit, and have people follow me around, carrying my passport, writing notes as I spoke about press statements, policies and which tie I should wear to tonight's gala with Oasis. I wanted to have a desk, a desk with drawers, and in those drawers I wanted a Filofax, with all of the important names and numbers of people who would listen to me. Me. Me. Me. Me. Me.

When I was three years old, not long after Tony won his first general election, my mum found me in the living room alone. I was standing on my red chair. This is a chair my mum had just bought me, and it went with a little red table, a table which I usually sat at to draw my self-portraits. But when my mum found me I was speaking to the empty room, throwing my hands around.

'What are you doing, Grace?' my mum asked me.

'I'm making a speech, Mummy!'

I wonder what my speech was about. Perhaps it was about how I was the best at speeches and how Tony should no longer be granted the right to make them. Or any other powerful man. Perhaps it was about my proposed law banning anyone but me from making speeches. I wanted little girls to be granted the same power that men had.

When I was seven, the Putins were due in town. Do you know the Putins? Vladimir? The Russian guy? Vladimir was coming with his family for an official visit. That's what world leaders like to do. They like to go to another country to get their dick sucked (metaphorically, of course – I don't want to be sued, or injected with Novichok) by other world leaders. They expect a whole song and dance when they come to London. They want a state dinner at Buckingham Palace so they can go back home and tell everyone that the Queen is a lovely old lady who loved them.

So Vlad was coming to London with his family: Mrs Putin, and their daughters, the Putinettes. And this was when he had only just got into power in Russia, and people were beg-friending him because they thought he might be a good one to be mates with. My mum told me about his state visit. I didn't know who Russia was, let alone Vlad.

'But what's so special about this guy?' I asked.

'Well, he's important right now, darling.'

'Am I gonna get to meet him?' I asked my dad. He laughed.

'What's funny?'

'Oh, you're being serious. No, Gracie. Probably not.'

But actually, I kind of did. While my dad was tasked with looking after Vlad while he was in town, my mum and Cherie were tasked with taking Mrs Putin and the Putinettes around London, and all of us 'children' were going to go with them. I got it. I was being put on the kids' table. While the men got to go and talk about important stuff like holidays and fast cars and nuclear missiles, I was set to go up the London Eye – and I'm not saying I didn't wanna go up the London Eye; it just didn't really seem justified that I wasn't allowed to have access to the big red button.

I dressed up for the big day. I was wearing a Nike tracksuit with Nike trainers and a Nike cap. When we got to Downing Street my mum took us up to one of the nicer rooms at Downing Street. You know that scene in *Love Actually* when Hugh Grant is dancing to 'Jump' and he bumps into one of his secretaries? The room looked just like that. And Vlad was on his way. We were all quietly mingling, waiting for the big entrance. Putin's wife and daughters came in with a general look of Dakota Fanning. Then Tony and Vlad walked in. You can always sense when someone has power, can't you? You smell it when they walk into a room, like a bitter perfume with too much coffee in it. They speak loudly, with an air of shut-the-fuck-up, knowing you will shut the fuck up and you will listen to them. They walk tall, even if they're short (or very, very short in Putin's case); they walk like they're on stilts. That's power.

The vibe in the room was very Freshers' Fair. Lots of nervous smiling but no one knew who to talk to. I wanted to talk to Putin, but he didn't look like he wanted to talk to anyone. I was used to politicians fussing over me and saying how cute I looked, but Vlad looked like he never said that kind of thing even to his own daughters, so I doubted he'd be nice to me. He walked right past me, and I realised how tiny he was. Like, seriously tiny. Wow, how can a man this small be so powerful? It gave me hope for myself.

Putin looked so miserable, though. While Tony and Cherie were boring him talking about paintings of Churchill, Vlad was nodding while his translator told him what they were saying, or not. I love imagining that the translator was just mistranslating what they were saying for fun. But Vlad didn't look like he did fun. Vlad didn't blink once. He looked like he wanted to leave. And then, all of a sudden, my dad announced that they were leaving to go into an important room, and they all left. They didn't even say goodbye. There was no 'Vlad, meet Grace, she is also a very powerful person' moment. The men with the power went off, and the door was shut before I could get in.

I was furious about not being invited into the important room. My dad had always made me feel like his equal; he'd walk into a room, and he'd come straight over to me. That gave me a certain level of confidence. In a room that the Prime Minister, his teeth and his bodyguards were in, I would feel more important than the Prime Minister. But then, at the same time . . . I wasn't invited into the rooms that powerful people were going into. And that was a blunt reminder that I wasn't the Prime Minister, and I probably never would be.

Standing outside that closed door was a complex place to be, because in one way I did feel superior to people in politics, because I thought I wasn't posh and they were. I know this sounds absurd. But my dad's personal campaign in our household was to make sure we were never posh – that just wouldn't go down with him. I was taught that posh was an accent. Posh was what school you went to: Eton, Winchester, Cheltenham Ladies' College, St Paul's.

My dad, who wasn't born posh, set himself up against these posh people. He wasn't born working class either, but he'd grafted to get where he was by then, in the most powerful place in the UK. And he hated how full of posh, privately educated people politics and the government were. Even though he was now part of the establishment, he wanted us to think we weren't. When I was ten he told me I could go out with whoever I wanted as long as they didn't wear a signet ring on their pinkie and think skiing and football were on a par.

So we were powerful – well, actually I wasn't, but my dad was, and in my head that meant I was by default. But we weren't posh. And yet I was somehow entitled enough to think that I should have been invited into a meeting with Tony Blair and Vladimir Putin when I was seven and wearing head-to-toe Nike, baseball cap included.

I didn't link these two things: that my sense of entitlement to be in that room actually came from the fact that I'd been born into this particular family, which meant I was already in rooms with the Prime Minister as a child.

One of the saving graces of my life is that my parents sent me and my brothers to local state schools. Shout out, Mum, for being a loyal campaigner on this issue. Mainly, I'm grateful for this because going to state schools really prevented me from turning into an absolute dickhead. I mean, can you imagine how entitled I would have ended up if I'd gone to a private school? Sorry if this offends anyone who went to a private school, but statistically, according to a personal study I conducted between the ages of four and twenty-five, people who go to private schools are more likely to end up being dickheads than people from state schools. Some examples: Boris Johnson, Jacob Rees-Mogg and David Cameron. Absolute dickheads, who all happened to go to the same school: Eton.

I've met Boris Johnson once. At a Miley Cyrus concert. Sorry, I'm so clumsy – can't believe I just dropped two names at once there. It was 2009. I was fourteen, Miley was sixteen and at the peak of her Hannah Montana phase. And Boris Johnson was the comical meme-inspiring Mayor of London.

Perhaps still guilt-ridden at how he'd missed so many of my birthdays by this point, my dad had got me and Emily tickets to go and see Miley Cyrus for my birthday. So we were in a box at the O2 arena, because . . . if we're talking about privilege, that's a great example of how my privilege and nepotism worked. And so we got to the box, and not long after we arrived Boris Johnson walked into that same box with his daughters, who were just as excited to see Miley perform as we were. While my dad chatted to Boris, we made fourteen-year-old small talk. What school do you go to? That kind of thing. They were at Bedales, which I'd never heard of. Emily and I told them we were at Parliament Hill School for Girls – they'd never heard of that either.

Watching my dad and Boris Johnson speak, I just thought my dad was much more impressive than theirs. He was handsome, cool and looked like he had his shit together. Meanwhile, Johnson looked like a supply teacher. He was so disorganised-looking. When he spoke he was out of breath, and his voice was so pompous. At one point he asked me how I found it having Alastair Campbell as my father, which is rich coming from him, and when he spoke little bits of spit fell on my face.

I didn't get time to answer his question, because suddenly Rob – the guy who had got our tickets for us – asked if we wanted to go backstage and meet Miley before she went on. My dad said no, because he was worried about being photographed with Boris Johnson. But Emily and I begged him, so, again probably because he still felt guilty about all those missed birthdays and the fact he got me a colouring book for my thirteenth birthday, we headed down to our fate.

When we were walking down, my dad and Boris Johnson were leading the crowd, as I guess they were the main attractions of this meet-and-greet. They were the London Eye and the Big Ben. Boris was probably going to use meeting Miley as a press opportunity for him, appealing to the youth, being seen with the Queen of Disney – it's a clever tactic. I was both happy and jealous at the same time. Obviously happy that I was meeting Miley, but jealous that it was being done for Boris Johnson and not me and Emily.

We got to the spot where we were told to wait for Miley, right next to the stage entrance, in a concrete tunnel.

Miley appeared, tiny and gorgeous, in a leotard, her boobs propped up – she didn't look nervous at all. Sixteen-year-old Miley, who was about to perform to 20,000 people – how did she do it? She got introduced to Boris. 'Hello, Mr Mayor,' she said in her strong Tennessee accent.

'Hello, Miley, how great to meet you,' Boris said. 'And this is my deputy mayor.' He pointed to my dad.

'Hello, deputy mayor,' Miley said.

I didn't appreciate this joke.

We all got a photo with Miley, and then she went out on stage to a crowd of screaming kids who couldn't believe they were seeing her in the flesh. I was annoyed that Boris Johnson had taken meeting Miley as a joke. Those screaming kids out there would've given anything to be there.

But then the thought also crossed my mind. Why was I any more deserving than he was? I wasn't any more special than the kids who were out in the stadium waiting for her to come on. But somehow I and Boris's kids had been there, backstage, meeting Miley Cyrus.

I might have doubted the fact that I was posh back then, but I couldn't deny the reality of the nepotism that had allowed me to meet Miley Cyrus, or, even now, has probably helped me get to the position where I'm writing this book.

I could look down on Boris Johnson's kids all I wanted for being posh. But I was there in the same room as them. I was getting the same picture taken with Miley Cyrus that they were.

Boris Johnson is someone who oozes privilege. He is a white man who went to Eton. He's never properly been held to account for being racist, misogynistic, homophobic or Islamophobic. Even the fact that he won't disclose how many children he has show's how bloody easy he's got it. Can you imagine if a woman prime minister refused to say how many kids she had? The whole country would be calling her a slag and giving her the boot.

But by looking down on him because I thought I had no privilege of my own, I was massively missing the point. Boris Johnson is not a knob because he went to Eton. He is a knob who went to Eton. But because he went to Eton, he can get away with being a knob. Having seen him close up, my assessment is that if he didn't have the background he does, he'd struggle to get a job serving drinks in an O2 hospitality box, let alone as the latest Etonian prime minister. Did you know that Eton, the school, has produced three times more prime ministers than the Labour Party has ever had? That is a REAL, hard fact.

I could sit here slagging off Etonians for the rest of this book, but I won't. Just because I know there are people out there with more privilege than me doesn't mean I don't have to acknowledge the power structures that I've benefited from. In the past few years, 'checking your privilege' has become a phrase that privileged white people use as a badge of honour for how they can publicly recognise that they've consciously or unconsciously been benefiting from a system at the expense of others. This feels like a bit of a cop-out. Checking your privilege is a good first step, but saying that isn't enough. We can all do more to dismantle white supremacy.

Even though I am still a ripe young peach, I feel ashamed that I realised all of this so late in my life. This shame is one of the few in this book that completely belongs in me. I thought that because I went to a diverse school in London and my parents are left wing that I didn't need to learn about my white privilege. I'm ashamed that even in writing this I know I still don't know everything and I still haven't done enough.

Not to sound too serious, but when you realise the power structures you've benefited from, it becomes easier to properly unpick how you're going to change those systems and better society. There's no pat on the back at any point during this process. This is probably why so many men in politics haven't done it – because they need instant gratification all the time. But as I, and you know from Vlad and the lads, if you don't assess your power and privilege, you are a dangerous person.

FAO DUA LIPA

Hi Dua,

It's me, Grace Campbell. I hope you're really well. You probably remember me – I was in the year above you at Parliament Hill School. I had curly blonde hair and braces for about forty-five years. I've sent a picture of me just in case you forgot.

I've just realised how creepy that sounds. Pictures in the post are creepy, I agree with you on that one. This isn't fan mail, though. I mean, I absolutely am a fan. I listen to *Future Nostalgia* from start to finish whenever I hoover my flat . . . Sorry, that was a lie, I don't hoover! But I love your music. I love dancing to it, #inmycalvins, while I vape.

It's really amazing to see a Parli Girl dominating the international music scene. You're so mega and you deserve every single piece of success you've got. You're talented. You're kind. You're generous. You're hard-working. You're political. You're fashionable. And you're just so cool. Your music is like private jets and feminism in neon colours. And your voice? A spiced rum and coke. My favourite.

I know we weren't good friends at school, but I can remember you were always singing in the corridors. Singing in the toilets. Singing in the queue for food. We were bearing witness to the birth of a superstar. We were there when you were becoming the popstar Dua

Lipa. But instead we all found your singing really annoying. Isn't that funny? You turned it into a world-moving career. You've won Grammys and BRITs. And here I am, still living with my parents, writing jokes about getting chronic thrush during my driving test.

I know I was a bit of a bitch at school. My memory is a bit hazy because I've smoked so much weed since then, but I know that me and my friends were bitchy to you and your friends. We thought that because we were a year older than you guys, we could make passive-aggressive comments about your clothes, or your hair styles, or the part you'd been given in the drama production. I'd just like to say on that, I am sorry, and obviously it goes without saying, I was severely wrong.

At school I seemed very arrogant, but I was deeply insecure. You might remember in Year 9, I got a wart on my nose. A big wart the size of a pea hanging off my nose. People tried to mock me for the wart, and so instead of letting them mock me, I just named the wart Rice Krispie, because that's what it looked like, and I turned it into a fashion accessory. I wasn't going to let a wart on my nose tarnish my reputation back then, but secretly I cried because, well, I had a wart on my nose.

Simply put, at Parli I let my arrogance and insecurities run away with me, and I apologise for all of that.

FAO Dua Lipa

I wanted to find out how you are. You seem like you're having a ball on Instagram. But we all know Instagram has a tendency to show only the good side of things. Has fame stressed you out at all? You became famous so quickly, which I'm sure has made you horny for yourself. But do you ever feel anxious? To go from normal life in North London to being a pop superstar that quickly. Do you ever wish you could just go to a pub and get ragingly drunk and piss in the street without anyone taking pictures of you? Maybe you don't care about that stuff.

Well, all I can say is that you have completely smashed it. And I know I was a warty tyrant at school, but I mean it when I say that I am very proud I went to the same school as you. I would obviously like to be the most famous alumni from Parliament Hill School, but you really deserve it more than me, so, IDGAF.

I hope we'll cross paths at some point. I have always thought I should get into song-writing, so let me know if you ever want some lyrics from me. I'll do mates rates, obvs.

Kisses,
J'adore,
Grace Campbell
xxxxx

I PUT THE MAD IN MADEMOISELLE

I remember my first few years of secondary school fondly with a smell. The smell of Mayfair Superking cigarettes. They sound so posh, don't they? Mayfair means you're doing very well on the Monopoly board, but when I started secondary school in 2005, Mayfairs were the cheapest cigarettes going. That's why, in the back field of our school, all the older girls smoked Mayfair cigarettes. I remember my first puff of a Mayfair in year 8. I felt like Leonardo DiCaprio in *Romeo & Juliet*. I didn't even cough. I know – everyone was like, who is this legend? But then, to be fair, straight after I had to run home and be sick. Of course, I had no idea how to inhale, which was a blessing in disguise – my baby lungs didn't actually have to take on the pressure of smoking.

I didn't properly get into drinking and smoking straight away. We were, after all, still eleven. But by the age of thirteen, smoking Mayfairs, drinking Glen's Vodka, and gossiping on Hampstead Heath was our religion. Before you start criticising state schools for this, I should point out that it wasn't the case for everyone at my school. Other people were busy harnessing their talents, Cc Dua Lipa. Also, most of the private-school kids I knew were up to far worse, and their parents were paying for that to happen.

It felt like my whole life had been preparation for secondary school. The summer before I started, I agonised for months over what backpack to buy for my first term, eventually deciding on a Cath Kidston one. *Très classique.* My backpack had a floral pattern on it that was also our tablecloth at home. It was a nice waterproof material, which was perfect for any Capri-Sun spillages that might happen. You might think Cath Kidston sounds lame, but honestly, she was like the Kylie Jenner of the Noughties.

Anna and I met on our first day at school. I noticed Anna before I met her. In a room full of twiglet-sized eleven-year-olds, Anna stood out. Firstly, because she looked twenty, not eleven, and secondly, she didn't look nervous at all. Maybe it's because she was wearing such an adult outfit. Our school didn't have a uniform, something which Anna didn't take for granted. On our first day Anna wore a bright-yellow Ralph Lauren knitted jumper, with yellow Converse to match. I admired the coordination. She had her hair gelled up in a quiff with two plaits. And the look was finished perfectly with a massive pair of fake diamond earrings. She looked like a female rapper at a golf club. And from the moment we were introduced, despite the fact that she looked more like my babysitter than my friend, we were pals. Anna was at the centre of my world, along with Emily (the non-drinker who you've met before), Nina and Ella (two new friends we'd met who were really sweet), and Tyler (who wasn't at school with us but was consistently part of this group).

Our year at Parli was particularly special because everyone was friends with everyone. It was a utopia of young women from different races, classes and backgrounds. There was a huge crew of girls who were in the Mayfair and Glen's clan. Every Friday we'd go up to the heath after school, drink vodka until we were sick and then go home at 7 p.m., convinced it was midnight, and pretend to our parents that we'd got food poisoning from a Tesco meal deal.

All we cared about back then was that we had mobile phones to orchestrate our plans, and that we all had personalised ring tones, bought with our pay-as-you-go pocket money. I had 'Where Is the Love?' by the Black Eyed Peas. I thought this set-up would be our life forever. I assumed it was the pinnacle of adulthood, being wrapped up in a bubble of female obsession.

There was barely any interruption from men. Even the male teachers at Parli had a softness to them because they knew that even if they tried to assert power over us, we would wear them down until they melted into a puddle of piss. Parli Girls were intense. We were competitive; we were confident; we were, without knowing it, fiercely feminist. The vibe at the school encouraged this. The teachers all wanted us to be feminists, and that spirit really echoed throughout the school, which again is something you can't pay for, and is almost certainly not for sale at Eton.

There was a boys' school next door called William Ellis. Willy Ellis, we used to call it. But for the first half of Year 7 we barely noticed the boys next door. They were like lift music: we heard them, but we never engaged. We could smell the waft of their pubescent BO from over the fence. We could hear their not-quite-broken voices from the playground. But we were so wrapped up in our love for each other, we didn't look at boys much. They seemed like an unnecessary item.

Being an eleven-year-old girl whose only interest was making friends with other girls did wonders for my confidence. I was obsessed with myself. I was obsessed with the sound of my voice. I was obsessed with what I saw when I caught my reflection walking past a car. I had so much self-worth it was exhausting carrying it round in my Cath Kidston backpack all the time.

NORTH-LONDON STATE-SCHOOL GIRL STARTER KIT, 2005

- Smokes Mayfair Superkings but doesn't know how to inhale.

- Carries a 'Just Do It' bag.

- Loves to brag about their school having the hottest teachers.

- Is obsessed with the performing arts.

- Does peace signs when posing for a picture.

- Only shops at NikeTown and Topshop.

- Loyally wears UGGs even though they've sloped inwards.

Then, when social media crept in, this all started to change. Social media was going through its adolescence at the same time as we were. MSN, Myspace and Bebo were well-established social networks, while Mark Zuckerberg was still in a dorm room in Harvard objectifying women in his campus – a venture that would one day become Facebook and make him even richer than Dua Lipa and more powerful than David Cameron.

IRL, girls still acted as though boys were infected jellyfish who would give us rashes if we went too near them, but online they were starting to close deals with them. Subtly, in the way that they do, boys started having a hold over girls at school. I hated this. It gave me a rash that I wanted to throw my own piss on.

Suddenly Charley and Koryn, my best friends from my form class, were talking about boys they were 'linking' with after school. I couldn't understand why anyone would 'link' with a boy, especially these two girls that I idolised. What would they get from 'linking' up with a boy after school?

Then Emily went and found herself an MSN boyfriend.

Sam was a William Ellis boy that she never once interacted with in the flesh, but now she was going home in the evenings to talk to him on MSN. Instead of bitching about her day to me, she'd go and bitch to him, behind a screen, about how much she hated the girl who sat next to her in English.

I was so obsessed with my friends that I didn't understand why we were now going to add an ingredient that might jeopardise everything. All teenage boys did was chat shit about which Xbox game they wanked over last night, and how many times they'd seen a boob in the flesh. But the hype of boys was being campaigned for everywhere. They were being marketed like Lucozade – take a sip of this boy, and you will become a woman. I hated the change, but I've always loved a trend, so I knew I had to buy into it.

One night I was on MSN when a message popped up. It was from **Matthew**. Matthew and I were friends at primary school, but since we'd started secondary school he'd ignored me outside the gates.

MVERFCKR2: Yo u likin parli?
BAYBEEBLUE: yh I luv it.
MVERFCKR2: Were du liv?
BAYBEEBLUE: Gospel Oak.
MVERFCKR2: I liv in QC. Lets link up 2nite.
BAYBEEBLUE: Ermm . . . I dunno, I'm watching stuff.
MVERFCKR2: I wanna c u.

BAYBEEBLUE: k but not 4 long.

MVERFCKR2: 10pm outside fongs. [Fongs was a Chinese takeaway at the end of my road.]

BAYBEEBLUE: Kk, cya.

I didn't tell my friends I was meeting up with Matthew – I knew they'd kill my vibe and tell me I was a mug for going out at 10 p.m. on my own to meet some random guy who, as Anna would say, 'wasn't even that fit'. Better to just tell them after, once we'd had a snog and I could say I'd done it, I've had my first saliva spreading kiss, so sue me! I'm a grown woman now!

I waited for my parents to go to bed. They're ridiculously early sleepers, so I knew this would be easy – 9.45 p.m. is always their cut-off because they're both committed to exercising in the morning. I put on my favourite hoodie from Gap over my pyjamas. At the time I thought nothing was more appealing than a hoodie from the kids' section at Gap. I fancied myself in that hoodie, so Matthew definitely would. I snuck out of the house at 9.57. It would only take me forty-five seconds to get to Fongs, but I wanted to leave extra time in case I got into trouble somewhere in those 70 metres from my door.

My street was asleep. I thought about how well behaved everyone else was being. All tucked up in bed at 10 p.m. Unlike me – I'm off out, little me, off out. God, I'm cool. But then suddenly, when I was walking along the street, I felt very little and realised that I could easily be kidnapped. What are you doing, Grace? You don't even care about boys. No, but you have to care about boys, Grace. Boys are cool. Boys are the new Furby. A bigger, pubescent, emotionally immature Furby.

I got to the end of my road, which I don't think I'd ever seen at this time of night without my parents. It's usually really busy, with people hustling through all day, but now there were no cars. I saw one man with a briefcase; he was powerwalking on his way back from his office job. He sleep-walked right past me, taking no notice of the eleven-year-old in pyjamas.

I got to Fongs two minutes early, which I was embarrassed about. I've always been an early person, but I was worried this would make Matthew think I was too eager. Ten minutes passed. No sign of him. I should have peed before I left. Twenty minutes passed. I checked my phone – a Nokia 3310 that used to be my dad's. No one had contacted me. Matthew didn't even have my number. Maybe he's died and one of his family members would find my number somehow to tell me. Why didn't I bring a snack? I'd love some raisins right now. Forty minutes passed. I panicked that my parents had realised I was gone and called the police.

I walked home, acting cool, because some part of me thought he might be watching me. By the time I got back into bed I was raging. My body was shaking. I took this as a big blow to the head, the vagina and the ego. How dare he stand me up? Did he see me waiting there outside Fongs and think, 'Nah, she's ugly, I'm gonna go home'? I should have followed my instincts. I didn't even want to go, but I thought I should because linking with a boy was the new thing.

I vowed to never like a boy ever again. But then there was **Tom**. I was thirteen when I met Tom.

Tom added me on Facebook after I met him at his own house party in Finchley. His parents were there making sure we didn't overdose on Smirnoff Ice and Party Rings. I was feeling confident one day not long after the party, so I took the plunge and asked Tom if he wanted to go to the cinema with me. Tom ignored my messages for a week and then replied saying he was dating a model. I couldn't believe it. How had I been stupid enough to think a thirteen-year-old boy would date me if he could get with a model? That night, the girls and I went to the heath and I got paralytically drunk. And in that moment I really didn't care about Tom at all. In fact, there seemed to be this incredible link between getting very drunk and forgetting about the boy who'd rejected you. Magic. I was a pioneer, again.

I thought **Toby** having the same name as the Tory teddy might be a sign. I was fourteen when I met Toby at the Anna Scher Theatre school. This was a drama school which I went to after school on Wednesdays. He was the most confident boy in the class. I was sure he was going to be as famous as Shia LaBeouf one day. One Wednesday after class, both of our mums were late picking us up, so we hung out in the park by Caledonian Road. We smoked roll-ups, still not inhaling, and I made him laugh by doing my impersonation of Kat Slater from *EastEnders*. He thought I was funny, so I took that as a sign that we were falling in love. By next Wednesday's class, I was ready to accept the invitation of being his girlfriend. But then, when I was walking into the class, I saw him holding Alice's hand. She was older than me, prettier than me, and they were clearly dating. Everyone thought Alice would be the next Kate Winslet. Then, a month later, we all got cast in the drama school's production of *Peter Pan*. Toby got cast as Peter, Alice got cast as Wendy. And me? I was cast as Nana the dog. 'Don't be upset, Gracie,' my mum said. 'Nana the dog is the first on stage – you basically lead the show!'

By now my body was starting to change. I was transitioning from a scrawny little girl into a hormonally charged young woman. I had grown humungous, ripe, juicy breasts. Overnight, I'd gone from not needing a bra at all to needing to shop in places like Bravissimo. Suddenly men on the street were laser focused on my chest like there was a Premier League match playing on it. And at the same time I got braces to finally attend to the huge problem that was my dental health. My teeth were like buoys in the sea; my mouth was full of 'mind the gap' puns. So I had breasts the shape of my head, which made my (metaphorical) head confused. My breasts got me more attention from boys, but not the boys I liked, and my braces made me think no one was ever going to want to be with me for longer than a snog, if that. How did I cope with the sudden change? Did I dedicate my time to dental hygiene and improving my mind? I did not. I went to parties, I drank Glen's and I waited for boys to make me feel good.

•

After Toby, there was **George**. I was fifteen when I met George. He was a boy from the year above at a private school near my school. George was the recipient of my first ever blowjob. I know. Can you hear the fireworks? Nope, me neither. No celebration needed. *Quelle surprise?*

George and I were hanging out on the heath one night, drinking Strongbow, when he suggested I suck his dick. He said it so casually, like he was asking me to put a pot of hummus back into the fridge for him. 'Suck my dick, please,' he announced. I didn't particularly want to suck on anything. I was worried my braces would tear his penis off. I knew that Anna had already done it, and she had braces, and she'd said it was really easy as long as you didn't breathe too much. But I was scared. What if I needed to breathe? I hadn't done any practice for this. George unzipped his trousers. 'Go on,' he said, so casually. So I took a deep breath and gave it my best attempt.

George pushed my head around for a few minutes, which made it even harder because I was trying to hold my breath, but this made me desperate for air. Once he'd had enough of me choking for air on his dick, he pushed me off, zipped his trousers up and then said, 'Is your friend Anna single?'

I didn't tell the girls that George had rejected me straight after I gave him head. It felt like a failure, and I think at this point failure in sex and love was only fine if it was collective; I didn't want to expose my personal failures to them. Instead, I just bragged that I'd given my first blowjob. 'YAY!!!!' they all replied in unison. I told myself I'd ticked off a major life moment. I was on my way to being an epic sexual being. But this experience of rejection immediately after I'd spent five minutes gagging on George's pungent dick made me feel like I'd just done an X Factor audition that was so bad it had gone viral. I hated myself so much that when I got home that night, I threw my UGGs in the bin.

If it sounds like my early teenage years were a non-stop party of dismal encounters with men, well done, babes – you have successfully guessed the theme here. But obviously in the background were all of the other exciting things that happen as a teenager. There were two distracting factors for me. One was that we made friends with boys, and that helped me a lot, and the second was that with those boys we started taking drugs and going raving, and that helped not so much.

Based on my previous experiences, I had been sure that being friends with boys was like trying to domesticate a rat. I think the difference now was that we'd become friends with boys from a co-ed school around the corner. Acland Burghley School was part of the group of four schools that ours was in, which meant we would all merge when we got to the sixth form. This group of boys we became friends with were proof that not all teenage boys were twats. I think this was something to do with them being in classes with girls. Effectively, they didn't just see girls as objects that you would one day pump sperm into.

This was how I met Jack, eternally my gorgeous gay best friend. Jack was, and still is, the best person to have around. Jack made all of us girls feel like he was the only man we would ever need, which was true. He was perfectly protective, and always made us feel validated. And then Leo, my very handsome straight best friend. Leo looks like a movie star; his vibe is James Dean. People can't believe that he isn't famous already, but maybe after this book he will be. You're welcome, Leo. The security of having these two boys in my life filled any void I had of male attention. It was even better, because I was at no risk of either of them rejecting me.

And so we had a big group of friends from these three schools who were obsessed with staying out late on the heath, getting high and arguing about what we thought we knew about politics. We started experimenting with drugs.

Because it was fashionable and fun, just like us. I smoked my first spliff with Nina and Leo on the heath and it was so badly rolled we ended up eating the weed. We started doing MDMA, which just made me want to snog, and ketamine, which made me never want to snog again. And then we started raving. This was incredible.

It was at my first rave that I met **Joe**. I was buzzing my tits off in a warehouse on a canal in Hackney Wick. My pupils were massive and my jaw had a mind of its own, which meant my mouth was gurning like it'd swallowed an electric toothbrush. Jack had jumped into the canal because of a bet, and while he swam around the murky water loving his life, this boy walked up to me. He asked if Jack needed help, and when I said nothing would get him out until he wanted to, we started snogging. Joe and I snogged for the rest of the time that Jack was in the canal. I don't know if you've snogged someone while you're on MDMA. It feels like you were born with a mouth that was supposed to snog the mouth you're snogging. Snogging Joe made me think that was the point of taking drugs: to be pushed up against a wall near a canal, and then kissing so hard we could taste each other's brains. Then, when Jack got out of the canal and realised he might get hypothermia and die if we didn't leave, Joe and I exchanged numbers. The next week Joe invited me to a party, and I thought I was finally about to get lucky. We'd get high, have sex, get married. He was the one.

As it turned out, it was there at that party he'd invited me to that he got with another girl in my face. I still got high, though.

•

I think rejection in all its forms is a very rude and ungrateful experience. By the time I got to sixth form college, I wanted to reject rejection. One day I sat down with my parents for a meeting to discuss my takeaway points about rejection.

'Guys,' I announced, 'I just keep being rejected by boys. I don't know what I'm doing wrong, but clearly I'm very unattractive.'

'No, Gracie, you're gorgeous. It's just because they can't handle you. You are . . . a lot . . .' said my mum. She then clearly panicked that this might upset me, because she added, 'In a good way!'

'Oh come on, Mum. If it's "in a good way", then why is nobody liking me, if it's so GOOD? If it's so good, why does every man I look at basically vomit in my mouth? This is clearly not a lot "in a GOOD way", because I do not feel good right now.'

'They're just immature. When you get older, they'll like you more,' my dad said, not specifying how old he meant. Are we talking ten years or fifty? This annoyed me more. He carried on, 'Don't worry about it Gracie, rejection is character-building.'

I looked around dramatically, and they watched me curiously.

'Sorry,' I said. 'Just looking for the character that I'm building right now. I can't see her. Character, where are you?'

They thought they were saying all of the right things, and maybe they were in a bigger-picture way, but at the time it didn't make me feel any better.

Rejection turned me into a bit of a monster. It unleashed my child-like demons. When I felt rejected, I was compelled to attack my body. Whether it be through drinking excessively or taking too many drugs and ruining my mental health, I always found a way to punish myself for the punishing experience of rejection.

I now started attacking my body in a new way. I had always had a confused relationship with my body. If my insecurities came to the surface, it was one of the first things they'd pick on. My mum's gorgeous figure made me feel much bigger than her when I was a teenager. I felt so big I thought I might squash her if I sat on her lap. I still did it, though, because I will do anything for attention.

I think I'd had body dysmorphia for a while. You might have no idea what this is – it's basically when your mind focuses on one aspect of your body and creates an optical illusion, distorting its appearance. In this case, my mind was attacking my body for being fat when I was simply existing. I used to look in the mirror after a meal and I would be able to see that my stomach was visibly getting bigger, and if I stayed there long enough, I convinced myself that my stomach was so big from that one bowl of pasta that I now couldn't eat for three days.

My weight became the fixture that I had to change. I decided that the reason I was being rejected so much was because I wasn't skinny enough – another pipe dream sold by the marketing gurus who want to ruin all young women's lives. I thought I'd lose weight, and then everything would fall into place.

I bought a book called *Skinny Bitch*, which is so fucking problematic in itself. And it basically told me to eat bird food and exercise for hours every day until I became so thin that I wasn't just a bitch, but a skinny one.

My friends were worried about how much weight I'd lost, and the fact that I kept fainting at parties. The girls would wake me up with a can of Coke and say, 'Grace, when was the last time you ate?'

And I'd reply saying, 'I had some bird food yesterday.'

So I'd lost weight, but I looked absolutely terrible, and I still thought I was hideous, and I still didn't succeed in love. This is only a brief venture into the hate that so many women, and men, and everyone else, are forced to place on their bodies. But speaking just for myself, rejection made me attack, and I attacked the two things that were closest to me: my mind and my body.

When we were finishing school, I think I was struggling to process how much of a failure I felt my teenage years had been. When I got that first message from Matthew back in Year 7, I thought I was going to embark on a pilgrimage of love like Marissa Cooper in *The OC* had done. I'd watched Marissa go from one intense 'I'll chase you to the airport' love to the next, and I thought my teen-age years would be filled with that same intense, I-would-die-for-you-love.

Unfortunately, the only thing I mastered in my teenage years was the art of being both too much and not enough all at once. I was lucky to have my friends, who would call me out when they thought I was dealing with my issues in a toxic way. Even though rejection made me feel like a half-empty glass of orange juice from concentrate, my friends made me feel like a vital organ in our system. To them, I was enough. Because of them, I was distracted from feeling like I would never be loved. But sometimes, because of the way we all lived, they also distracted me from realis-ing that I was using drink and drugs in the wrong way.

•

By the time I'd reached my early twenties, I had worked through my issues with my body. I had done proper ther-apy on my dysmorphia and my relationship with food. I hoped because of this that things might change for me. And they did, in a way. I started to get a lot of attention from men. My boobs had returned after their brief bird-food-induced absence. I'd learnt how to dress these juicy ripe grapefruits. And my personality, which had always put teenage boys off, was starting to turn men towards me. They were like Frisbees, for my teenage years they'd been running away from me, and now they were all coming back. Men a couple years older than me were starting to love the fact that I didn't flirt or play stupid games. But I kept meeting men who gave me the ick.

Like Hugo, the extremely hot six-foot-three man I met on the Tube, who was absolutely obsessed with me, but when I snogged him his mouth created a river of saliva and I gagged every time. There was also Robbie, the guy who wrote a new song for me every time I saw him. Even when I told him it wasn't working, he improv'd a song. Or Isaiah . . . the boy who loved to go down on me but always referred to my vagina as a mango, which gave me mental thrush.

And then I met **Will**. Will isn't his real name, but his real name was just as white and basic as Will. I met Will while I was at university in South London.

During this time, my anxiety was bad. So bad that I was leaving my house and going back to check my front door was locked on average 10 times every day. I'd just come back from Paris and started at a new university, and even though the panic attacks had stopped and the medication I was on was starting to work, I still had low-level anxiety all the time. Like tinnitus of the mind. I never quite felt I fitted in my body. When I'd put on a coat I could never feel whether or not the arm was going through the sleeve, because I was so detached from my body.

And alcohol was such an appealing distraction because, for a moment, I could forget that just that morning I'd convinced myself I had cancer in my elbow. But then the hangovers put my anxiety on speed. Hangovers are the most anxiety-inducing act you can inflict on yourself. Physically, you're dehydrated, which makes you anxious. You can't remember everything, and so your mind plays tricks on you about what you said and did. You question whether or not you still have any friends, because you convince yourself that last night you went on a rant about how much they talk about their boyfriends and now you worry they think you're a bitter old bitch.

I was stuck on a loop of being too anxious and then getting drunk to numb my anxiety, but then, as a result of getting too drunk, staying up till six in the morning at a house party, and the next day hating myself so much that the only way I could numb that feeling was to drink again.

I went to a lot of house parties then. I really loved house parties. They were the perfect medium for me because you could never get lost, and there was always a place to sit down and judge people with my friends. So one night I was at a house party in Peckham, where most of the uni students now lived. They weren't from Peckham, they just gentrified it and talked about it as if they'd brewed it in their garage. This was a particularly good house party. It had a massive living room with dramatic red walls, a DJ and a giant disco ball that I was mesmerised by. Then there was a huge garden with a bonfire going, where everyone was smoking roll-ups and doing laughing gas. I was with Jack and Emily, which was great because we have the gift of always being comfortable even when we don't know anyone at a party. I observed that there were a lot of fit people at this party. My anxiety was like Elon Musk's rocket on the way to Mars, but I was still desperate for a moment's attention.

I saw Will across the dance floor. He was talking enthusiastically to a group of people while he was dancing. There was something about him that I liked. He looked really . . . happy. Everyone else at the party was too busy trying to look cool and he just looked happy.

He also looked like he was on a lot of drugs. Charlie Sheen levels of cocaine – perhaps that was why he was so happy. I pretended not to notice him. And then I could see he was walking over to me. I pretended not to notice.

'Hey!' he gave me a hug. 'We've met before, right?'

'No,' I said.

'Are you sure?'

'Yeah, I have a photographic memory. I've never forgotten a face in my life.'

'I like you,' he said, 'something about you . . .' Why did I feel like he was looking into my soul?

'Yeah, I'm pretty special,' I agreed.

'There's something about your energy . . . I really like it.'

Usually I don't fall for this kind of shit. I am not anti-spirituality, quite the opposite. Now, I'm a yoga and meditation fanatic. But I've always found that people use talking about energy as a way of acting like they have superpowers, to con you into thinking they're more special than you by claiming they can see inside your soul. My old flatmate, Daisy, had a boyfriend who had added Rasta onto his name and had adopted elements of every form of spirituality into his life. He was spiritual in a pushy kind of way and used to constantly corner me in the living room, claiming that my chakras needed to be cleansed, when the only thing that needed to be cleansed was his sage-smelling breath.

But now Will was saying it, and I just needed to hear it that night.

'Do you take cocaine?' he asked. Another trait of faux-spiritual people is that they are always addicted to very unethical drugs.

'Yeah, of course,' I lied. Coke was the worst thing that I could possibly take then, now, or ever. Taking cocaine if you've got anxiety is just paying lots of money to give yourself a panic attack.

But he was drawn to *me*. That must mean something. We went up to the bathroom and he took a huge line of cocaine off of the sink. I watched him taking it and when his face came up he looked really ugly. He had this Voldemort vibe coming off of him. I didn't want to take any, but I didn't want him to know that.

'I'll just have a small amount, thank you.' He put it on my hand and I then waited for him to wash his hands and I blew it into the bath.

'I feel like this bathroom has a very retirement-home-in-Florida vibe,' I said.

Will turned around and laughed.

'These tiles – I want a three-piece suit with these tiles on it,' I carried on. 'I want to be Jane Fonda wearing these tiles.'

Will kissed me suddenly, maybe just to shut me up. It was a terrible kiss, but I felt hard all over my body. We snogged, properly, for a few moments and then suddenly my jaw locked and I bit his tongue.

'Owhh,' he said.

'Oops, sorry!' I pretended I wasn't embarrassed.

'It's okay.' Will looked ugly again. I can't explain it. He didn't look like the happy person I'd just seen on the dance floor. He cleaned up and left the bathroom without me. Once I'd sorted myself out, I came out of the bathroom and saw he'd started talking to another girl. I walked past with great confidence, went outside, spoke to my friends and decided to go back to Leo's for an afterparty. When I woke up the next afternoon, I turned this story into one where I'd lost my chance with someone amazing. It was all my fault. All because I'd bitten his tongue.

Weeks later, I added Will on Facebook. It was, after all, 2015! He accepted me, but then didn't say anything. I thought about him ~~sometimes~~ every moment of the day. I thought obsessively about our brief encounter and how he'd made me feel like the most important person in the world. I was so desperate to know if he'd thought about that moment since then, or if he just remembered me as the girl who bit his tongue.

Then, in the middle of the night, months later, he messaged me out of the blue.

'How are you, darling?' I hated it when boys our age used the word 'darling'. It reminded me of my mum and I never thought they were mature enough to pull it off. But he'd asked how I was. He cared!

I replied enthusiastically, 'I'm good, thanks! How are you?'

And then he was gone again. Nothing, for months. He was probably off with some skinny hippy woman taking magic mushrooms in a field somewhere.

Then I was at a house party in Camberwell one night, and I saw him across the kitchen. 'Grace!' he rushed over, coke all over his nose. 'I've got to talk to you. I've been needing to speak to you for so long!!'

'You could have replied to my Facebook message then,' I said, not caring about what that said about me.

'Yeah, I'm sorry, I was getting out of a really long-term relationship then, and I felt bad leading you on – I'm not that guy.' He snorted a lump of snot to the back of his throat. 'But it's all over now.'

I was pissed off. I'd spent months thinking that from one brief encounter and a Facebook message this clown was in love with me, but actually he'd been busy dealing with his own shit. 'Let's go to the toilet,' he said.

I hate coke. I hate coke. I hate coke. I hate coke. I hate me on coke. I hate Will on coke. I hate everyone I've ever known on coke. It makes people talk about themselves like they've just won twelve Oscars in one night.

But I was back in his spell. His energy was so intense; I should have known it could never endure for long. We went home together that night. And he stayed at mine for days after. We had sex. I liked him – so much so that I told myself the sex was good. But it wasn't what I wanted. Sex with an AI robot would have been more loving. Will didn't like to kiss me. He didn't really like to look at me, to be honest. And he was really into choking, which terrified me.

I don't even like wearing chokers, or turtle necks, because I hate things wrapping around my neck, so I'm not sure why I should feel differently about someone's hand pushing on my neck when I'm supposed to be turned on. But for some reason I kept sleeping with him. I wanted to recreate the way he looked into my eyes that night we met.

This carried on for months. He'd warned me he was never going to commit to me. He actually told me, on multiple occasions, that he didn't want to have sex with me, he just did it because he knew I wanted it so much. He was still rejecting me, but in more subtle, manipulative, cruel ways. My friends were warning me off him. Tyler met him once and the first thing she said was, 'I don't like him, and I don't like his *energy*.' He was treating me like his charity case, making me feel that I should be grateful to him for having sex with me. He'd come round, already wasted, and we'd drink and have these conversations that felt meaningful but were actually just about him, and he would never once ask me how I was feeling. And then we'd have sex and we'd wake up hungover and he'd leave.

And then one day, I'm getting my fanny waxed, and I get a message: 'I'm back with my ex. Let's go for coffee soon, though?'

I hadn't even asked him a question to prompt this. I was preoccupied with trying to get over my obsession with him. I was going on dates with other people to clear my mind. But he sent me that message because it was his pièce de résistance. It was his final act of violating me. He knew that he could break me, and he did.

I found his ex on Instagram. She was very tanned, very blonde, very skinny. The type of girl men like Will would move to Devon with to grow butternut squashes together. Of course they'd been back together for months, and he'd already been cheating on her with me, his charity case.

The problem with Will was that he hid behind this spiritual nice-guy act, and so his trash behaviour was much harder to articulate when it was happening, because he was so good at playing a lovely character.

This rejection was far worse than anything else I'd ever experienced. Everything before this was a meal at Pret. But Will . . . this was Michelin-star rejection. Hats off to the chef. Bravo. I felt like I had been poisoned. What had I done to deserve this? Maybe I was being punished for letting myself become obsessed with a coke addict who spoke at me about my energy instead of asking questions about me. I should have seen that when his face turned possessed after a line of coke, that was because he probably had the devil inside him already.

As with all of my other rejections, I buried myself in booze and my friends, without facing up to the fact that rejection made me feel like a rabbit that had been hit by a car on the M25. I should have addressed this. I should have confronted the fact that Will made me feel desperate, and he made me a bit tragic. They were both things I never wanted to be, so I drank to forget I felt that way. I should have found an alternative coping mechanism to deal with this rejection.

But it was the summer, and we were on our way to a festival, so I didn't.

•

My mental state came to a head in a field. A field in a place called Huntingdon, which is somewhere in England. Sorry if that sounds vague or offends anyone who is actually from Huntingdon, but unfortunately, when it comes to English geography, I'm like that girl who went on *Mastermind* and thought Greta Thunberg was a woman called Sharon. You might be thinking, 'Typical Londoner,' but actually I could win *Mastermind* on Scottish geography.

I was at a festival called the Secret Garden Party. A name that probably once worked when it was actually a secret garden party for a group of friends getting together in the summer. But this was 2017 and the festival had become so huge that it was its last ever year, I think because it became impossible to keep it a 'secret'.

So I'm in the field and I've just come to, out of a k-hole. This is a state you can get into when you've taken too much ketamine, the painkiller for horses that's been appropriated by humans who now use it as a cheap hallucinogen.

My mouth is really dry. So dry that I think I'm going to swallow my tongue. It feels like lots of little borrowers have come into my mouth with mini vacuums and they've drained my system of all the saliva so they can make it into a mini paddling pool for them and leave me choked.

I'm twenty-two. I am about to graduate from university. This summer, instead of thinking about the compounding noise that is filling my mind with messages of worthlessness,

I have decided to go to a festival and pretend I am a feral animal for four days.

I am in a new phase of my life, in that I have finally realised how attractive I am. This is a few months post-Will and I've come to terms with the fact that I have been going for the wrong type of man. I was too influenced by boys who were telling me what I wasn't, while I should be thinking about all of the incredible things I am. I've found a perfect hair routine to enhance my amazing curly locks. Every item of clothing I wear is perfect. I dress like the love child of Edina Monsoon and Vivienne Westwood. I look like a really good time. Like a piñata at a kid's party.

But on the inside, I am still a complete and utter fucking mess, also a bit like a piñata. If you hit me, I'll explode. My mind is a driverless car. I'm in the backseat, being driven by it, but I have no idea where the car is going.

While everyone else my age has been spending the last few years getting into relationships, I have spent them officially being rejected. Of course, you've heard about some of them, but there were so many more. More liars, more ghosts, one man who had sex with me and then while he was still inside me told me he was engaged. I was done with them all.

Tara is lying in my crotch. Her long brown hair is floating down my legs, it looks like I have a hairy head of pubes.

Tara is a new friend of mine who is also from North London. Tara and I knew of each other throughout school but we fell in love with each other last summer at a reggae festival in Spain that we both love. We had a friend romance, which I wish I knew then is the best kind of romance. Tara is a gorgeous, hilarious, very observant person. She never misses a beat and so we spend most of our time laughing at things we notice. Now, Tara is a huge part of all of our lives, and it feels like she's known all of us forever.

Tara has just watched Jack and I do a balloon. Nitrous oxide. 'Laughing gas' is what the bad salesmen call it. I think they're naming it all wrong, because laughing gas, in my experience, doesn't make you laugh. It makes you resent the moment your father came in your mother's vagina. It makes you ask questions like, 'Why do we even have legs if we can't walk on water?' It makes you question how much everyone around you likes you and whether or not you're just friends with them because you're from the same postcode. But the perk is that this feeling only lasts for fifteen seconds. It's like an existential crisis in the form of an Instagram story. Fifteen seconds and then you're back, and you're thankful for that moment in hell because it makes you feel grateful for real life.

So we've just done a balloon. And now I want more drugs. But my friends have told me they're not letting me drink or take anything else because they're 'concerned'.

'About me?! How can you be concerned about me?' I am annoyed with them. They're patronising me.

The festival had started off more promisingly. I was feeling gorgeous and fashionable and popular, my triple-ring confidence formula. But on the first night I bumped into Will and his tanned girlfriend. I hung out with them for far too long in an effort to prove that I was 'fine' with the whole situation. I actually at one point went to the toilet with his girlfriend, and I stayed in the stinky Portaloo while she did a shit. I was so 'fine' with this situation.

Since then I had been on a non-stop mission to be the fun piñata who had no connection with her conscious mind. I had tried to do anything I could to block out the loop in my head repeatedly telling me I would never be loved. I would never be loved because I am unlovable.

All of North London was at this festival, and that meant I kept bumping into some of the people I'd banged. But I didn't even care. I was with Jack, and Anna, and Tara, and that was all that mattered.

Then, on the Sunday morning, I had woken up alone in my tent to a text from a man, Joel, who I had recently gone on my first date with back in London.

Joel Bumble: Yo! How are you? Hope you're good. This week has been mad. I worked twelve hours every day, except Friday, when I worked fifteen hours. And it fucked me up. So this morning I took a long introspective look and asked myself what's important, what I want, what I need and what I don't. And I put dating in the category of what I don't need at this stage of my life. So although I had a great time with you on Saturday, laughing and dancing, meeting your friends, and fucking, I think it's the right decision for me if I don't see you again. Hope you understand. Thanks for a wonderful Saturday night, Grace Campbell x

Grace Campbell: Looooool, ok.

I couldn't believe I was now being rejected again by someone I didn't even like and hadn't thought about once since I'd been on a date with him. We'd been on ONE date together and the fucker thought I was so obsessed with him that he needed to go out of his way to dump me? But here I was, minding my own business in a tent in Huntingdon, being rejected again. I'm so disposable they should probably just throw me away with the tents at the end of the festival.

I left my tent. Anna had already gone out, so I went to find her. I ignored the fact that my stomach was telling me I needed to eat. I hadn't eaten anything for three days apart from magic mushrooms. I ignored my hunger and went and found my friends, who were already seshing. This was the rainiest festival I'd ever been to. It rained non-stop the whole weekend, and by this point on Sunday, the mud was in our bones.

I didn't know it, but I was craving insanity, and I was doing everything I could to lose my mind. But my friends know me. They can see the difference between me having a good time and taking it too far.

'No,' says Jack, 'you are done for the night,' once we've done the balloon and I tell him I want more drugs. I huff and I puff, but neither he nor Nina nor Anna nor Leo nor Tara gives in to my manipulative tactics.

We go to the Lost Woods and there we're reunited with the whole of our North London extended group. Everyone I have ever known from primary school, secondary school and sixth form, dancing in the torrential rain. I'm so fucked. I'm looking around at this group. I've got with a few of you. Why has nothing ever worked out for me? I'm going to be alone forever.

I decide I need a drink, so I walk off alone. I bump into Nic, a boy I used to fuck. He's with his new girlfriend, who is nice in an Australian kind of way. I can't deal with the awkwardness of being with yet another person who ghosted me, with his new girlfriend.

But they're offering me ketamine. And no one else will let me have ketamine. Sure, why not? I take it, and politely dance with them for 120 seconds (I count). Then I find my way back to my friends. I might as well be in a simulator at the Science Museum. Nothing is real. I'm dancing, but I have no limbs.

I'm dancing with Jack and Leo. I need to stop. I need to stop. 'Grace, stop,' I hear my therapist say in the back of my mind. 'Stop what you're doing, eat something.' But right now my therapist's in the really cheap seats of my brain. She's all the way at the back, and I can easily ignore her from up here on the stage. I don't stop.

When I'm in a really bad place, I think about how sad people would be if I died, and what a historical event my funeral would be. I think about the bright colours people would wear. I think about the fact that my friends would somehow get Damian Marley to come and sing at my funeral. Maybe Katherine Ryan would do a set – wouldn't that be great? I think of all the people who would come. Friends from all over, ex-lovers who rejected me and have now realised they love me back, now that I'm gone.

Doing this makes me feel better because it reminds me that I am worth a lot to other people, that my death would be a huge loss to the world, not least because of this book. Plus, I like the idea that I am so well connected that Damian Marley would definitely say yes.

•

When I woke up in the Lost Woods at Secret Garden Party to see everyone I've ever known since I was twelve crowded around me, shouting at each other about what they should do – well, that was the closest I've ever felt to that funeral fantasy being real. I had collapsed onto the floor, in front of all the people I've ever known.

Anna was at my feet watching the paramedics approach me. She was crying, realising that she was going to have to be the one to tell my parents that I was dead. Alice, a new friend of mine who had helped me get through university, was leaning over me, calling my name.

And Leo was squeezing me hard. He had picked up my limp body and was trying to find life in me. He whispered in my ear, 'Just give me a squeeze if you can hear me, Grace.'

'Is she squeezing?' Anna asked.

'Not yet. Grace ... please, squeeze me back.' I could hear him. I squeezed him back.

'Okay, she squeezed back.'

Then I whispered, 'Leo, have I shat myself?'

THINGS YOU SHOULD DO WHEN YOU GET REJECTED

- Call your friends.

- Print out a picture of the rejector and set it on fire.

- Have a few drinks with your mates to take your mind off it, but not so many that you wake up anxious and alone. Three drinks max.

- Unfollow/mute the rejector on all forms of social media.

THINGS YOU SHOULD NOT DO WHEN YOU GET REJECTED

- Start hanging out with the person who rejected you and their new partner because you're 'so cool with them'.

- Take so many drugs that you nearly die in a field in Huntingdon.

●

After my near-death experience at Secret Garden Party, I was very low. I mean, I'd literally gone into the bank of my brain and robbed it of all its serotonin, so partly it was chemical.

But also, this was a meltdown that had been pending for a long time. It had been creeping up on me for a year or so. And now I'd put myself in a position where I had to confront my chronic fear of rejection. I love putting the word chronic in front of things like that – just makes it all sound so much more serious.

But I did need to address the fact that my fear of rejection made me take things too far. On occasions, when I've been rejected, I've even wet the bed – I'm here breaking down the taboo of adult bed-wetting! I decided to stop taking drugs and to try my best to eradicate the party lifestyle for at least six months until I felt mentally stronger. And it did help. It didn't eradicate the bad feelings, and it certainly didn't make me a green-tea-drinking, drug-free saint. But it gave me some perspective on how I was using coping mechanisms to deal with my insecurities.

Making that connection changed my life, literally. It made me see booze and drugs in a completely different light, and since then I have never got so fucked that I've done anything I've regretted. That's a big deal for me.

And not long after this I started doing stand-up. Which is a great job to do if you need to overcome your fear of rejection, because you'll find you can be rejected by many people in one night.

Now *that's* the type of character-building my dad was referring to. In deciding to do stand-up, I was accepting that not everyone was going to like me, and that's fine. I was accepting that I would be 'too much' for some people, and that's great, because I could recognise that those people aren't my people and then move on.

When I took my first show to the Edinburgh Fringe, which is a month-long arts festival in Edinburgh that happens every August (unless there's a global pandemic) and is supposed to be the be-all and end-all of comedy, I got very good at rejection.

I wrote a show called *Why I'm Never Going into Politics*, which was about growing up in politics. It was an obvious show to write because I had loads of stories, but also because I knew people would see the title of the show, see who my dad was and buy tickets. Maybe I should have just called the show *Nepotism*.

I'd not been doing comedy for very long, so I didn't understand how brutal Edinburgh is in terms of reviews. I'd not prepared for this at all.

The run started off amazingly, and my first few reviews were great. Then I got one from *The Times*, which I shouldn't have read, and since that fateful day I've never googled myself, and don't plan on doing it ever.

The man who reviewed me was someone who clearly dislikes my dad. He focused the whole review on how privileged I was, on how much I was tail-coating on Daddy's name, and that I was an aggressive and preachy woman.

I wish I could have seen in that moment that this guy was someone who was just never going to like me. The show was full of jokes about privilege and nepotism. He'd missed the point. But I couldn't see that clearly enough at the time.

It sent me to a really dark place. I went to that place where I went after Matthew, George, Will and everyone in between who had rejected me. But instead of wanting to have a drink or get really fucked up, all I wanted to do was show this man that he was wrong. My mum and dad were in Edinburgh when I got this review and saw that it was getting to me, so they checked out the guy and discovered that he went to Eton. Bingo! It was all I needed to know. I now don't care what he thinks.

I think my dad might have been right when he said rejection is character-building. All those years have prepared me well for my current career. Now, rejection just makes me want to be better, so I can make dickheads feel small.

And to any men who went to Eton and might be reviewing this book, you probably don't like me or my book. And that's fine. I probably wouldn't like you either. But do take care and best wishes for the future.

DICKHEADS ANONYMOUS

MATTHEW, TOM, JOE and WILL (Grace's rejectors) are at Dickheads Anonymous, a support group for recovering dickheads.

TOM

Welcome to Dickheads Anonymous, guys. My name is Tom, and I am a dickhead.

BOYS COLLECTIVELY

Hi, Tom.

TOM looks at MATTHEW's shirt.

TOM

That's a nice shirt, Matthew. Where is it from . . . Gap?

MATTHEW

No, it's from Zara men's.

TOM

Zara men's! How European of you.

MATTHEW

Thanks.

TOM

So, last week, Matthew, you really opened up to us . . . and I feel a lot of progress was made. You admitted that you

have had a tendency to stand women up in the past
because you've been so insecure about your penis size . . .
How have you been feeling since you let these feelings out
last week?

MATTHEW

I've felt better since then. I actually went home and
measured my penis. Turns out I had a bit of dysmorphia
about it. It was more like an avocado.

JOE

Your dick's the size of an avocado?

MATTHEW

The length of an avocado, yeah.

JOE

What about the girth?

TOM

That's great news, Matthew. Good for you. Avocados are a
superfood, too.

MATTHEW

I think I need to remember what my piano teacher used to
tell me: it's not the float in the boat, it's the motion of the
ocean.

TOM

I think it's size of the boat.

MATTHEW
What?

TOM
It's not about the size of the boat, it's the motion of the—
never mind. What about you, Joe?

JOE
Well, I've been thinking a lot about what I said last week.
I've been trying to work out why I cheated on Sophie,
my ex.

TOM
What have you been thinking?

JOE
I realised that the girl I cheated on Sophie with reminded
me so much of Sophie when I first met her.

TOM
You think you cheated on your girlfriend because she
reminded you of your girlfriend?

MATTHEW
Why didn't you just get with your girlfriend?

JOE
Because it was like Sophie in the early days, when she was
all unhinged.

TOM
I'm afraid that's not a real excuse.

JOE
What do you mean?

TOM
You can't excuse cheating by saying that the person was like Sophie 1.0. The beauty of this group is that we know that once you come here, you're on a journey towards never being a dickhead anymore. The closer you get to your truth, the further the dick will be from your head.

TOM hints towards WILL, who has been silent up until now.

TOM
We also have a new member today. Boys, this is Will.

BOYS COLLECTIVELY
Hi, Will.

TOM
Will, do you want to share something with the group? Why have you come here today?

WILL
Same as you guys, to talk about Grace Campbell.

MATTHEW
We're not here to talk about Grace Campbell.

TOM

Well, we can today, if Will wants to share something.

JOE

Wait, who's Grace Campbell?

MATTHEW

She's Alastair Campbell's daughter.

TOM

Okay, she's also a comedian in her own right, Matthew.

WILL

Well, she never made me laugh. She just talks about fanny farts and edibles and how jealous she was of Tony Blair.

MATTHEW

Well, comedy is very objective.

JOE

Ohhhh, I remember her. Yeah, she was a lot. She had crazy eyes.

WILL

Was??? She's still a lot. That bitch is writing a book about me without my permission.

JOE

Are you a comedian, too?

WILL

No, I'm a chef.

TOM

I don't think she's writing a book about you.

WILL

Of course she's writing a book about me. She's gonna
write all about how I fucked her over. She's so self-
absorbed it makes me want to get on my knees and lick
the pavement.

MATTHEW

I'm confused, how do you know her?

WILL

We used to fuck. It was always casual, but she didn't think it
was. I mean, I should have seen it coming. When I met her I
could see she was a little crazy. But at first I found that
energy sexy.

TOM

Mmmm, fetishising mental health. Not filling me with
hope.

WILL

But she was just into me so quickly, and she was too honest
about that, and I don't like it when people decide they're in
love after meeting me a few times.

MATTHEW

That doesn't make any sense.

WILL

Why? Why would I want to know instantly that I can have someone? What's fun about that?

MATTHEW

Because honesty is quite healthy.

WILL

So are avocados, but I don't eat them.

JOE

Well, not after today's update.

TOM

Look, now that we're on the subject, I know that we all have experiences with Grace Campbell, and we don't need to talk about it. But I'll admit it, too: I was a dickhead to Grace. I lied to her. I told her I was dating a model because I didn't want to go to the cinema with her.

WILL

God, that's brilliant, bet that made her feel like shit.

TOM

But it wasn't like that. I liked Grace as a person, but I was in love with my neighbour and I thought I had a chance with him. Then he rejected me, so I guess that's karma. Anyway,

Dickheads anonymous

Grace and I are friends now. I met her again years later, after I'd come out, and I think she's a boss.

WILL

She's not a boss. She's a dickhead. I thought that's what this group was about.

TOM

This group is for us.

WILL

For us to talk about what a dickhead Grace Campbell is. I thought this was a support group for people who are being fucked over by her shitty little book.

MATTHEW

No, this is for us to talk about how we've been dickheads to women.

WILL

I'm not a dickhead.

JOE

You're wearing a Supreme hoodie.

HEAD IS OVERRATED UNLESS YOU'RE IN LOVE

Trigger warning: Hi, babes, this chapter has references to rape. If you think you might be triggered, please don't feel you have to read it. Love you x

Have you ever been sent a dick pic by a stranger on the Internet ... and looked straight at that picture and thought ... 'Wow, I'm gonna marry that man one day'? I'm genuinely curious about this! Have you ever opened a message to see a pixelated pic in your inbox that you didn't ask for and then eloped with the owner of said penis? Please do get in touch if you are that anomaly. Because, in my experience, that is not what happens.

When my inbox is invaded by a dick I don't want to see, my clit turns into sandpaper that's so sharp it cuts my fanny flaps. Men, listen to me: you are never going to get laid, loved or validated by sending pixelated pictures of your dick to strangers who didn't ask for it, okay? Please stop that!

But dick pics are just one of the myriad things teenage girls are told to accept as a part of life. I got sent my first dick pic on MSN when I was fourteen. I accepted most usernames back then in case they were girls from school that I wanted to be friends with. This one was from Mario5666443. Mario5666443 was definitely not my age, as I could see from his profile picture. He looked like a middle-aged man. He'd sent me a picture, and at first glance I couldn't understand what it was, because it was 2007 and it needed time to buffer. So I waited patiently for it to load, and when it finally did I remember squinting hard, because on first glance I couldn't tell if it was a fish or a dick. It reminded me of my old goldfish, Sparkles, who I'd won at my cousin's school fête and accidentally killed when I was eight. I sprayed deodorant in the fish tank when it smelt.

But then I noticed that on this fish there was hair. Hair like poison ivy, climbing up to the balls. The foreskin frowned furiously at the top. I'm sure it knew this wasn't an appropriate picture to be sending a fourteen-year-old, and it was pulling an angry face at its owner. It's not the dick's fault that his owner is a creep! That was my first sighting of a whole penis posing for a picture, and it terrified the shit out of me.

That same year, I was wanked at on the Tube by an adult male. I was on the Northern Line, alone, coming back from Anna's house. The carriage was empty, and the man, who was in his forties, was sat opposite me. I noticed he was fumbling in his trousers while he was looking at my innocent fourteen-year-old breasts. And then he started doing the motion that I recognised because so many people at school imitated it. He was smiling at me, like my dentist does when he's about to stick a needle in my mouth and he's telling me it's not going to hurt.

Teenage girls grow used to unsolicited dicks flying around them like pigeons in Trafalgar Square. Dicks online. Dicks offline. Dicks graffitied in school. Dicks are advertised to us like a new state-of-the-art gym. They look unappealing, but you know eventually you'll have to indulge, even though they don't seem very female friendly. And then, when you start interacting with sex, you feel like you're then on trial at the gym. You don't really know how anything works, and the induction was a bit brief, and you're watching everyone else use the machines and they look like they know it all, so you feel you have to pretend that you know it all, too, even if you're risking dropping a 10kg weight on your hand.

When I started getting with people – in my case boys, because I've always been pretty heterosexual – I always did everything to the max. *Par example*, the first time I snogged a boy, I didn't just snog one boy, I snogged six boys in one night, because that was the vibe of the house party we were at. The girls and I were having a competition: who could snog the most boys. Unfortunately, that was the night I contracted the life-long disease and impediment mouth herpes, which has since given me the bane of my life, cold sores. My mum had no idea this is how you get cold sores, from snogging, and so I had to be the one to tell her that she, too, is a carrier of mouth herpes.

But snogging loads of people and contracting mouth herpes is fine if that's what you want to do and you're organised enough to use Zovirax. However, we're not always that lucky, are we? We're not always given the luxuries of consent or boundaries. Because we think that words like 'no' or 'I don't like that' are such violent boner murderers, and if we say those words we'll end up in frigid prison, and once you're labelled as frigid at school, you can never come back from that.

The problem with my generation was that while we weren't learning much about sex at school, we were learning about sex online. In my experience this was mainly boys who were watching low-quality porn on Pornhub. I've since spoken to some of my male friends from sixth form, and they said they started watching porn at eleven; they started soft, and then a couple of years in they graduated to some pretty hard-core stuff: gang bangs, BDSM, choking and lots of double penetration. I don't think you can totally blame them for this, but the reality is that they had access to the lived-out sex fantasies of fully formed adults while their minds were still forming. So boys took this porn as a demonstration of what they had to do, even when they hadn't even learnt the basics of sex, they were trying the hardcore. But that's like trying to make a cheese soufflé when you haven't even made cheese on toast.

Our parents had no idea what was on there, so they couldn't protect us from it. This was before the time of internet safety and child locks on computers. It was the beginning of the Internet as we know it. Adults actually believed that their sons were upstairs doing their home-work, when in reality they were more likely wanking for the fifth time that day to a porno about a son and a step-mum having sex in the kitchen. Boys really thought they knew all about sex because they'd been watching these videos for so long. In reality, they knew nothing. They were just good at making us feel like we were amateurs because we didn't have dicks.

Not long after I was wanked at on the Tube, my friends and I were hanging out with a group of boys we'd become friends with at a house in North-west London. It was a hot summer's night so Emily and I were lying on the grass in the garden, half-asleep. One of the boys we were hanging out with came out into the garden and lay between us. He thought we were asleep, so what did he do? Obviously, he tried to put his hands down our pants in an ambitious attempt to turn us on. I mean, that was a stretch. We both shuffled, so he stopped, but not completely. Next, he started stroking our chests, trying to feel up our boobs. We both shuffled again and he stopped. Afterwards, Emily and I found this really funny, and in a way it was. He was trying to have a threesome with us when he was a fourteen-year-old virgin.

This kind of touching became a normal part of adoles-cence. If you shared a bed with a boy, in a non-romantic way, you had to be prepared for the fact that they would touch you up. Or worse, they might try to put their hands on your vagina, and in that case you'd have to be good at getting them to stop without confrontation. Because you didn't want to offend them.

How sad is that? We thought we needed to spare these boys their embarrassment, at the cost of us feeling shame.

It's made to seem like the natural thing for girls to do. We make excuses for other people's behaviour. We're traumatised, and instead of putting the shame on the people who have violated us, we attack ourselves for all the ways this could have been avoided.

The invasive touches were obviously bad, but they were nothing compared to what was to come. Being stroked on the tit while I was 'sleeping' was the foundation for how men were going to ruin me. So now, if you'll let me, I'll tell you about some of the times when I've had to deal with some very challenging experiences in my life. And again, this chapter contains references to rape and sexual violence, so please do stop reading if you think you might be triggered.

'YOU'RE BUTTERS ANYWAY'
Said the teenage boy after he got rejected

When I first gave head to that boy George in Hampstead Heath, I know I didn't want to do it. I wasn't ready to have a half-baked dick shoved down my throat, but I decided it was time I did. I can remember him pushing my head down and then pulling my hair around. I felt like I was getting my hair cut by a trainee hairdresser. But I presumed this was what was supposed to happen when you gave a blowjob, so I accepted it. And afterwards, the only shame I felt was that I had been rejected by him. My head wasn't good enough.

The next time it happened was a terrible sequel to part one. Like *The Hangover Part II*, I felt robbed. The boy, Finn, tried to force me to give him head in a playground. When I said no, his dick got harder. I think he thought we were playing a game. He forced me to put his dick in my mouth. I was choking, of course; everything about me was tense and closed, so my body rejected this foreign entity in my mouth. I was crying, because I felt terrified that I would suffocate. Devastatingly, I think this made him enjoy it more. Obviously, this was what he was expecting.

I used force to pull away and jumped up. 'What you doing, babe?' Finn said. He still thought I was going along with it.

'I'm going home. Don't follow me because if I tell my dad about this, he'll fuck you up,' I said.

'I'm not gonna follow you, you're a slag and you're fucking butters anyway.'

Of course this was his reaction. 'You're butters anyway' was every boy's comeback when they got rejected. They think that, in making you feel ugly, they can stop caring that they've just been rejected. They are insecure creatures who don't like hearing the word no, and so they have to minimise you. It's very transparent. It's a bit like when Donald Trump just screams 'Fake news!' at every piece of bad press that comes out about him. It's a defence mechanism, and thankfully I could see it as that on the night when I ran home and vowed never to give head again.

I stuck to this vow. Well, sort of. I got really good at getting out of giving head. I used a theory that I have also applied to making tea. Stick with me here. Whenever I've worked in offices, I've employed the same tactic to get out of always having to make tea. On my first day of work, I offer people a cup of tea and then intentionally make them a bad, piss-weak brew, so they'll never ask me again and I can live my life making teas for myself. I applied this same method to head. Sometimes I did it badly so people would never ask me again. Other times I would just say, 'You don't want my head, I'm terrible at it.' I was delighted with myself for creating this method, but I never really thought about why I'd had to.

'BE FLATTERED HE WANTED TO'

Says the older man who normalises abuse

When I was fifteen, I went to a house party in Dalston. My period was due, which was, then, the only time I got spots, so I'd gone to the toilet to top up the concealer on a spot on my face. The door opened and a boy called Marcus came into the toilet without my permission.

Marcus was tall and he looked like a creep. His eyes told you he was a creep, even if the rest of his face was trying to be charming. I'd only met him that evening. Marcus was friends with a guy at the party that I wanted to get with, so I had been making him laugh so that he would speak highly of me to his friend. But Marcus had clearly misinterpreted the situation, and he'd come into the bathroom with one intention: to claim something.

'Are you okay?' I asked. 'I'm nearly done.'

'I'm good, wanted to see what you were doing.'

'I'm putting concealer on, I'm nearly done.'

'You're not done,' he said. 'I just got here.'

I was confused; he'd literally just seen me and his friend flirting. But he was obviously jealous and wanted to stake a claim. He put his mouth close to my neck. I noticed he had chapped lips and wanted to offer him some Blistex from my bag. But he was preoccupied. He pushed me against the wall – he thought he was being sexy.

'Marcus, get off me.'

'Make me.' I pushed him off me. He thought this was a game, too, and he was stronger than me. He pushed me back against the wall and licked his fingers with a tongue that was sharp like the end of an acrylic nail. He put his fingers up my vagina, showing me he didn't know what he was doing. I didn't do anything. Well, that's not true; my face reacted, because it was painful. I waited, frozen, hoping that the stiller I was, the sooner he would stop. He pulled his fingers out to spit on them some more and saw that they were covered in blood.

'Bruv, that's so fucking grim – you've got blood on my fingers!' He started washing his hands. 'Nah, that's disgusting – you should have fucking said you were on your period – what the fuck!? How am I gonna get this shit off??'

And it was just like that. He had walked into the bathroom when I was doing my make-up to cover up a spot, and somehow I was the one who walked out of the bathroom ashamed.

'YOU NEED TO STOP GETTING SO DRUNK'
A friend once said to me

The worst thing happened in Paris. Of course it was Paris. The cursed Paris. Only bad things happen to me in Paris. Sorry to people from Paris. *J'adore* your language, but Paris has never been lucky for me.

I was unhappy about my life in Paris, but the only positive was that I had a lovely friend there from Leeds called Ruby. Ruby was always trying to cheer me up. We'd go out to bars, drink wine, smoke roll-ups and talk French to random people, until we got bored and went home to watch *The OC*. It was a welcome distraction from my anxiety.

One night we were out at a bar in Belleville, which was one of the rare spots that hadn't been heavily gentrified yet. We were in the smoking area and Ruby and I started talking to a group of French guys who were all a bit older than us. I was showing off my amazing French vocabulary.

'*J'adore. J'adore. J'adore. J'adore.*' They were j'adoring me.

The next thing I remember is waking up in a room. A spacious room with nothing on the walls – no furniture, really. There was just a shoe rack with loads of pairs of trainers on it. Where am I? I can feel I'm in bed with a man. I could feel his body near me; he was facing away from me, with his body leaning on the wall. I identified him as one of the men in the smoking area. Okay, fine. I've slept with him.

But I didn't remember how I'd got there. Is Ruby here, too? I could feel that sex had happened. You always know, don't you? Even if you can't remember it, you can feel it, especially when you haven't enjoyed it because you can feel the mental bruises from where it hurt.

I shook the man hard to wake him up, but he didn't budge. I had a strong sense that he was actually awake, because I could hear in his breath that he wasn't relaxed; it wasn't sleep breathing. I would be an incredible informant. I assumed he just wanted me to leave, so I took the hint. I got out of the bed, put my clothes on and left.

I mapped my way back to the nearest Metro station. I was pretty far away from where I lived, in a sort of suburb area of Paris. As I walked, I started piecing together my night. We'd met those guys. I couldn't remember anything after that. I remembered eating yoghurt. I remembered him giving me a pot of yoghurt. Why would he give me yoghurt? Am I a baby?

When I was waiting for my train I got a call from Lloyds Bank saying that someone was trying to Western Union themselves 500 euros from my bank account. I looked in my purse. My card was there, but the cash I'd had the night before was gone.

Had this man robbed me? Okay, now I felt like I was in *Taken*. I would make a joke about calling Liam Neeson, but that guy's racist, so no thank you, Liam, goodbye to you, don't need your help.

I got on the Metro. I looked like a proper state, and no one in Paris likes an English girl doing the walk of shame on the Metro. They will give you looks that they think are subtle, but you can tell they're smirking while simultaneously texting their friends to say they've seen a disgraceful English girl on the Metro.

But today I didn't have time to think about how I was being judged. How had I got so drunk? I wasn't drunk at the bar at all. But I'd woken up at 4 p.m. at this guy's house, which was the latest I have ever slept in. I'm not a late sleeper, ever, and at this time my anxiety meant I was lucky if I got four hours of sleep. Okay, so he must have tried to Western Union money from my bank while I was asleep. There was definitely quite a bit of cash in my purse, but I could have spent it. On what, though?

Could he have drugged me? How? I mean, it is quite weird to give someone yoghurt when you get back to their house. It was peach yoghurt as well, with bits – *je déteste* yoghurt with bits.

I went on Google: 'Can someone drug you in a yoghurt?' Google results tell me you can in fact overdose on yoghurt. NO. I typed into Google: 'Can someone put a drug in a yoghurt and then drug you . . .?' I didn't want to type what I thought might have happened.

I phoned Ruby. I told her what had gone down. 'Babe, it sounds like . . . you were drugged . . .'

'Drugged and robbed,' I said. I had to laugh, because otherwise I would start crying, and the only thing worse than an English girl doing the walk of shame on the Metro is an English girl crying on the Metro.

'HE'S JUST LIKE THAT'

Said a woman who was excusing a man's pervy behaviour

Some years later, I woke up in my bed and someone was having sex with me. Not someone I'd invited back to my house (still not okay). Not my boyfriend – no, no (though still not okay). I had gone home alone that night to the flat that I lived in with a friend. I was a bit drunk, but I can remember brushing my teeth – alone. I got into bed – alone. I watched an episode of the US *Office* – alone. I fell into a deep sleep – alone. And in the middle of the night I woke up, and someone was having sex to me. Not with me. To me.

This person was someone I knew, and he was someone I had slept with once before, but the last time we'd had sex was over a year before this incident. He was someone who, for as long as I'd known him, had been very tactile. He would always casually stroke my bum when we were out. He would always stroke my boobs when he'd hug me hello. But that was something I'd accepted as a personality trait of his.

I should have seen that as a red flag. If someone makes you uncomfortable, it's a red flag. If a guy is happy to continuously make other people feel uncomfortable, he probably wouldn't see the problem in ringing on my bell in the middle of the night for so long that my flatmate let him in and, on finding me in bed fast asleep, getting into my bed, uninvited, and having sex with me.

I obviously blamed myself for this. I thought I must be such a slag that he thought he could do that. I can't imagine him thinking he could just turn up uninvited to many houses and fuck someone while they're unconscious, but he thought my house was like a cheap and easy Airbnb.

I resent that I have spent so much of my precious mental energy thinking about what I could have done to avoid this situation. That for a long time I thought it was my fault.

But it wasn't, and it never will be. Soz, but I'll never be soz.

'BUT I THINK I NEED BOUNDARIES'
My mind said to my body

Rape is like a harrowingly bad trip on magic mushrooms that you never quite recover from. That might sound pessimistic, but in my experience, that's just a fact.

Sexual assaults obviously vary. Some you know are happening at the time, some are much more subtle – perhaps it's with a friend, or a partner. Others you don't realise it's even happening to you because you're so not with it. Let me be clear: all of these scenarios are equally, abhorrently and violently wrong. They can all fuck you up for an indescribable amount of time.

I have friends who have told me in recent years that they've only now realised they were raped when we were younger. By our fucking friends. This is how acceptable this kind of behaviour was when I was growing up. And now, I'm part of a whole generation of women and men and non-binary people who feel like squatters in their own bodies because of the actions of someone else. Because other people think it's acceptable to invade someone's entire existence as if we're made of rubber.

I've made excuses for other people for too long. I've shamed myself for at times being so promiscuous that I thought I deserved whatever I got. But let me tell you this: being a slut doesn't mean you should ever be raped. You are at liberty to sleep around if you want to – it is never synonymous with what I think is one of the cruellest things that can happen to someone. No one, ever, deserves to be raped.

Talking about these experiences makes me feel too vulnerable to articulate. But the shame that I've felt since experiencing this kind of abuse is one of the deepest that I know. It's a form of shame that I'll probably have to live with forever, albeit less frequently.

I wanted to talk about my experiences because I know that some of you reading this will have been through similar things yourself. Because, to be bleak, a lot of you reading will be my age, and I know that you will agree when I say that boys weren't taught shit.

And to those people who have been through this: it's not your fault. As you and I know all too well, we have been the guinea pigs of a broken generation when it comes to sex.

And to all of the people who aren't being believed right now, can I just say that I believe you. I know what it's like when people who you've told about your own trauma carry on accepting the perpetrator without any kind of confrontation. And that simple act undermines every ounce of pain that you're carrying.

And to all of the people who are too scared to even say what's happened to you, don't ever in your life feel you have to talk about it. You don't owe anyone this story. You can still be loud and legitimate talking about sexual violence without having to talk about your own personal experiences.

And finally, to the perpetrators. The ones who think they're a changed man because they're now reading a book by a woman who's riding a dick on the cover. To the men who think that because they haven't done anything 'rapey' since uni, they're cured of this. If you know that you've done something in the past that falls into this pretty broad category of abuse, and you haven't yet taken any account-ability for it, then shame on you. You've potentially ruined someone else's life, and you haven't even stopped to think about your own actions. Take responsibility. See a thera-pist. But don't expect the person who has survived your abuse to accept your apology or make any of this process easier for you.

The thing I hate most about all this is that we, the victims and the survivors, are the ones who carry the shame. I hate that the people who have done these things to me don't walk around with the same sickening, self-loathing feeling that I do. I hate the fact that they probably don't think about it when they're in the shower. I hate that when they have sex with someone they actually love, they don't have flashbacks to the times when they were forced to do this same act with someone they hate.

All I can say is that it does get better. I don't think the memories can ever be eradicated from your mind, and sometimes they will intrude when you're having a good day, but these occasions will become so infrequent that you'll soon realise just how far you've come.

I have felt very angry at men for a lot of my life, and honestly, after the experiences I've had, I never thought I'd be able to trust one again. I resent the fact that they learnt about sex in the most dangerous way and that, as a result, my generation of women were treated like goal posts.

'HEAD IS GREAT WHEN YOU'RE IN LOVE'
Me to Anna

I didn't think I'd ever properly enjoy sex. Obviously, the Dickheads Anonymous crew weren't a great endorsement. And then the impact of what happened to me during that time doesn't really need to be explained further.

But it wasn't all terrible and I really don't want you to think that trauma makes you an irretrievably traumatised person. While these things were happening, and they were really difficult, I was also having so much fun in so many ways. And while I had given up on finding someone who would make me feel completely safe in sex, I hadn't given up on extreme sexual pleasure. I was having very memorable one-night stands. Like the time I had sex in the garden of the Vatican, for example. Or the one time I shagged a Tory.

I was also wanking every day, at midday. There's something about the middle of the day that really turns me on, so thank God I WFH, because otherwise I'd be written about on many online forums.

I was ready to happily commit to a lifelong humping session with my vibrators. I wanted to marry my bullets. Maybe I'd occasionally cheat on them with someone I'd met in the queue of a kebab shop in Kentish Town after a night out. And that would have been me. But then I fell in love.

Now, I'm not trying to say that the solution to getting over sexual trauma is falling in love. That would be very unfeminist of me, and also I don't believe that to be true at all. Young women are sold a lie that once we fall in love, all of our other problems vanish. That's a pipe dream, likely conceived by the same man who decided that being shat on by a bird is good luck. When you fall in love, all of the same problems that you had remain, but if it's good love, the person you're with helps you carry some of the heavy trauma and they show you the positive versions of intimacy.

I did meet someone who helped me do this.

I was twenty-four, and finally completely in love with myself. I'd been seeing a therapist for a while, which is a privilege in itself – I wish everyone who's got trauma could see a therapist. You have no idea how trauma stores itself up in your body and comes out as triggers when you least expect it, and therapy helped me process all of this. So I was finally starting to work through my shit. I was still a very mentally unstable young woman, but I could finally hold the power of my sexuality in my hands. After ten years of being out of sync, my mind and my body were now in the same time zone. But I wasn't sold on love. I thought I'd loved people before. I thought I'd loved Will at the time, but that wasn't love, it was desperation.

Then I met Bae, as I will call him in this book. My Bae; the first man to really make me understand love, and it's something I will always be grateful to him for, whatever else happens in our lives.

I met him by chance. Well, not by chance at all; we matched on a dating app, which makes it sound less romantic, but there is no shame in meeting people on dating apps. Don't listen to your friends who have been in relationships since they were fourteen – they'll all end up unsatisfied. Dating apps are amazing.

We met on an app called Hinge. Have you ever used it? Anyway, I had been on Hinge for a month or so but had never met anyone from it. I matched with Bae when I was on holiday in Turkey, drinking an espresso martini pretending I was Eddie in *Absolutely Fabulous*. I saw the message and made a mental note to reply, but when I got back to London the mental note had been lost.

Bae messaged again. Okay, he persists. We start chatting. He's funny. The night before we go on a date he sends me a voice note. He's not only funny, his voice is also extremely sexy. This bodes well.

The night of the date came and I was suddenly panicked. For the last few years I had kind of sworn off men. I had decided they were only good if they were gay, or if I was having a one-night stand with them. I didn't want to go and meet another man who would eventually end up in Dickheads Anonymous. But Anna forced me to go, on the basis that 'You just never know. And if it's awful, you can leave.'

First dates are always so weird, especially when you've met them on dating apps. You have no idea how much of a freak they're going to be. I'd been on so many bad dates before this one that I'd learnt you had to always go in knowing what your escape route would be. It would make you less nervous going into the date if you always knew you could get out.

Twice I left dates within minutes: once when the guy told me 'Campbell isn't a very Scottish name'. This offended me to my core, because Campbell is the most Scottish name, and I didn't like that an American was mansplaining my heritage to me. I pretended to get a call saying that my parrot had escaped, and I left.

The other time I went on a date with a man who told me he didn't vote in the referendum to leave the European Union. When I expressed my fury at this fact, he told me that it was fine because 'I can vote in it next year'. So I checked my phone and pretended my friend had gone into labour, so I had to leave.

So I always went to dates knowing what my excuse to leave would be. When I went on the first date with Bae, my clause to leave was going to be that Tyler, who I was living with, was locked out. All I'll say is that within ten minutes I knew I didn't need an excuse to leave. We were both desperate for reasons to stay.

I remember the first time I saw him, walking into the bar in Shoreditch. I hid behind a lamp post and got a proper look at him before he saw me. He was so much fitter than his pictures. He was tall, his hair had a fresh trim and he had a warm, handsome face. He was wearing Clarks Wallabees. My favourite shoe. Shoes are the main thing I judge a man on, and he had passed the test.

When he first smiled at me as I walked into the rammed bar, I felt like I was being held. In minutes, I was making him laugh telling him about my friendship group. And all we did that night was laugh. And snog. And laugh. An hour into the date, I texted Anna: 'Omg Anna he's the best!! He's so funny so gorgeous so nice omg you are going to love him.'

I wasn't wrong. All of my friends did love him. The first time Anna met him, she titled him Bae. My Bae. He was different to anyone I'd ever known. He was confident, but with absolutely no ego. He was charming, but with zero elements of creep to him. He was cute, and he was fit. But most importantly, we were obsessed with each other. I could have watched him do anything, and it would have been better than any episode of *The Real Housewives of Beverly Hills*.

I think a lot of this was because he was six years older than me, so he'd shed a lot of the adolescent trash before I met him. We met at the perfect moment in our lives.

We'd had very different lives. Bae's family is Nigerian, and most of his family are doctors. He was born in Lagos, and they moved here when he was nine. He went to boarding school, which I'm fascinated by, and is a very loyal South Londoner, which has meant too much time is spent on the Victoria Line.

Bae is a Labour voter but isn't obsessed with politics. This was perfect because it meant he wouldn't be obsessed with my dad. I needed Bae to be obsessed with me only.

'How would you feel if I spoke about you on stage?' I asked him once when we were in bed.

'Obviously I would love it,' he said.

I've discussed the most intimate details of our sex life on stage. I've spoken about his dick, extensively, even when his family – including his mum, who's one of the most incredible women – was in the room.

At the beginning I tried to sabotage our relationship multiple times. On our first date I slept over at his, and as we were walking past Brockwell Park to go to the station, I pointed at the park and said, 'I once shagged a random guy in there.'

Stuff like that I'd do all the time. I hate admitting this, but I think I was testing him to see how much he liked me. Don't try that, guys, it's not fair on the other person.

What Bae had to learn about me was that I am an explosive person who's dealing with a lot of emotional trauma all the time. I had to learn that I couldn't control him, or his reactions, and that you do have to compromise, hence why so much time is spent on the Victoria Line. Being with Bae has mellowed me out – a little bit. You'd have to ask him for further comment on that.

I'd had sex with a lot of people by this point in my journey towards realising the point of it. And this was it. He wasn't like the pricks. He listened, and we communicated. I had never felt so loved by anyone. Don't get me wrong, one-night stands can be great, and I love the stories they provide. But sex when you're in love? I mean, it's like eating a Michelin-star meal at home.

But I still had work to do on my sexual trauma. I had spoken with Bae about what I was going through, and he just got it. About six months into our relationship, I asked him if he'd noticed that I'd never given him head. He was clever enough to know that there was something else going on there, and so he never asked or put any pressure on me to do it. 'Yeah, but I assumed you didn't want to,' he said.

And it was in that moment that I realised I could enjoy head again. Finally, I had someone deserving of my good blowjobs. Not my fake bad ones. My good ones. I loved this penis, and the owner, so much, I was turned on by giving him head. I felt at home doing so. I felt safe doing it. Sex was different now that I enjoyed giving head. It felt like I was finally happy with the way I was having sex.

Plus, some people have their best ideas in the shower, but I have mine when I'm giving head. Like that line. I had the idea for that line while I was giving head.

It's not that falling in love resolves your sexual trauma, because it doesn't. But what meeting someone like Bae made me realise was that I'd been exposed to so many pricks, and not enough of them were people who appreci-ated other people's boundaries. I finally knew what it felt like to be with someone who protected my sexuality like the security at Selfridges on Boxing Day.

•

Before I wrote this chapter, my anxiety was riding high. I knew it would make me anxious, because that's what trauma does. It comes out in crazy ways, like thinking I have cancer or that a mosquito bite on my leg is going to kill me. My anxiety convinced me that in writing about this, I would make myself unlovable again. Writing this chapter made me a living nightmare for everyone in my life, especially Bae. I was unreachable and needy; I was emotional and angry.

Writing this made me sad for younger me, and for younger you, and for young people right now. I hate that, as I'm writing this, I know for sure that this stuff is still happening to people, and that it's going to leave a long-term mark on them, all because no one thought to sit us all down and give us a proper sex education.

I never want anyone to feel ashamed for as long as I did for something that they didn't do. I hope that in reading this you can see why this shame should never live in you. The shame is on the people who did this to us.

Sex can be so messy, and everyone makes mistakes, but when we don't teach kids about boundaries and consent, we're setting them up for catastrophic failure.

GIRLS WANK TOO AND FANNY FARTS DON'T SMELL

So, it should be perfectly clear that nothing good comes from a sex education strictly from Pornhub. But what else is out there, I hear you ask? You might be wondering how I became such a sexual sage, and who was my teacher? It didn't happen overnight, babes. Here, I offer you my journey of sexual education. And I'm sure you won't be shocked to hear, it's pretty messy.

When I was a virgin, I had endless unanswered questions about sex, such as: can you get pregnant from swallowing cum? Or, what happens if the penis pushes against your bladder and you wet yourself?

When I was at school, sex was either taught biologically (as in, we learnt how a baby is made and what chromosomes are), or it was taught through gossip ('Did you hear about Lilly and Daniel having sex on the bandstand?'). The actual facts about the rest of sex seemed to be encrypted in a secret place, and I needed to know more. So began my education.

I'm fifteen. I am in the waiting room of the Brandon Centre, an infamous sexual-health clinic in Kentish Town. My hair is unkept and scraggly, like a horse's pubes. I wear crop tops all the time. My midriff is always available to be seen by the naked eye. I don't care that my tummy isn't flat. If a top isn't cropped, I'll crop it. I've got an addiction to cropping tops. Call me Britney. I've cropped some of my dad's Burnley football shirts. I've cropped my mum's Vivienne Westwood tops. Neither of them were happy about it, but I just told them: cropping is my religion.

Anna, Emily and I have made the journey up the road from our school to go to the Brandon Centre, and this is a huge moment for all of us.

To be finally in the waiting room of the Brandon Centre feels like I've made it in this life. I've known about the Brandon Centre for a while now. It's free for anyone under the age of twenty-five to use. It's where everyone who's having sex or wants to have sex goes to find out all the mystery intelligence that we need to know. Its clientele is young, gorgeous and deeply naive. And that's why we're there. We are desperate to be part of the Brandon Centre's social scene.

A middle-aged, kind-looking woman enters the waiting room. 'Grace Campbell?' she says. This is my moment. I follow the woman through the beige corridors – I presume she's the doctor. She welcomes me into her suite. There's a bed, a desk, some leaflets – it looks just like a doctor's room, but it feels more exciting. I absorb it all. My first time.

'Hi, Grace. My name is Helen, and I am the doctor at the Brandon Centre. Is this your first time here?'

'Yes, I'm excited.'

Helen is amused by this. I like her. I can tell she's very unjudgmental.

'So, how can I help you, Grace?'

'So, I got fingered last night, and I wanted to get a pregnancy test,' I announce.

'Did you have sex?'

'No, but I'm worried he had sperms on his fingers, because he had his hands down his trousers before.'

'Oh, okay.' She smiles, and I feel like we are connecting. I'm making her smile. I love it here.

'It's virtually impossible for you to have got pregnant,' Helen reassures me.

'Can I still do a test?' I was desperate to say I'd done a test to Anna and Emily.

'Well . . . this happened last night?'

'Yeah, at 8.45 p.m. On Hampstead Heath, near the dog ponds.' I wanted to show off some more, but I shut my mouth.

'I wouldn't be able to do a test anyway, it's too soon. Have you had sex before, Grace?'

'No, not yet, but I've done everything else.' This is the teenage oath of a virgin who wants to be taken seriously. She smiles again.

'Okay, do you plan on having sex soon?'

'I hope so.'

'Right, well, I'll give you some condoms then, and when you want to come back and discuss other forms of contraception, you let me know, okay?'

Anna, Emily and I left the Brandon Centre with a bag full of condoms each. We went straight to Starbucks in

South End Green for a Frappuccino, where we dissected my fingering session of the night before.

For three years to come, I didn't use any of the free condoms Helen gave me. Because sex was still an exclusive members' club that I wasn't cool enough to be part of. But I would still go to the Brandon Centre routinely, because that was a members' club I could be a part of; it was the fan club for sex. I'd go to see Helen for some reassurance on my vagina-condria. Like one time, when I was seventeen, I went to see Helen because I thought I had a baby stuck in my vagina. Still a virgin, but Google said it was possible. Helen took a look at the baby in my vagina and told me it was an ingrown hair. 'Go home, take a bath and wait till you can pop it.'

Every time I left the Brandon Centre, Helen had made me feel safer about my future sex life and reproductive organs. Plus, I always gained another bag of condoms to add to my stash. I was a sex fanatic who had never had sex.

The waiting room at the Brandon Centre was always full of groups of girls who had the same idea as we did: to make the pilgrimage to find out more about their bodies.

This also meant the waiting room was full of drama – another reason why we were hooked on this place. When I was sixteen, Anna and I were waiting to see Helen, and in the waiting room with us were two girls who looked a bit younger than us. They looked like they presented morning TV and had woken up at 5.30 a.m. to do their hair and make-up. I respected how done up they were for a sexual-health clinic. One of them had really long, straight blonde hair, and the other one had a shoulder-length bob, which made her seem very mature. I assumed the two girls were friends because they were painting each other's nails and talking loudly about someone called Daniel, who the blonde one was fucking, it seemed.

They got called in before we did, and after they'd both been seen by Helen they exploded into the hallway, screaming at each other. 'I knew you were fucking him!' said the blonde one. 'I said this all along when we were on the heath, you fucking slag!!! And you've given ME chlamydia.' I had to assume they had both fucked Daniel. Blondie punched her best friend hard in the middle of her tanned face, and then her friend punched her back in her tit. 'You punched me in the fucking tit, you bitch!' I wanted to be part of the action.

This drama all played into the idea we had of sex. That sex was dramatic, sex was outrageous, sex was going to write all of our storylines in years to come. But when we were sitting listening to the two girls fight about chlamydia, sex felt so far away from our reality. They were the first people I'd ever encountered who actually had an STD, but still we were more focused on watching them fight than asking if they were okay.

At the start of our time at the clinic, our innocence meant that all the information we learnt seemed so detached from us virgins that it never quite stuck. In the waiting room, where Radio 1 was always playing on an old radio hidden in the corner of the room, there were leaflets and posters about everything sexual-health related. Gonorrhea. Chlamydia. Pregnancy. Abortion. Contraception. The information was there, but we cared about appearances too much to ever pick up a leaflet about genital warts. Because what if someone saw me reading about genital warts? And then a rumour would spread throughout North London that I, Grace Campbell, had genital warts. Do you want me to say genital warts again?

During those years of going to the Brandon Centre, Helen answered all of my questions about sex. She reassured me that I wasn't dying . . . all the time. I thought that in the act of going to the Brandon Centre, I was doing all I could to learn about sex.

I thought I knew it all before I'd done it. I thought I'd walk into sex like I walked into my French oral GCSE exam: '*Bonjour, c'est moi! Je suis pret!*' (Hello, it's me, I am ready). But *non, non, non*, sorry, it just never happens like that.

•

I'm eighteen. I'm still wearing crop tops – that trend isn't dying any time soon. And I now *finally* have a genuine reason to go to the Brandon Centre. I've come today because I've decided I need to go on the pill. Mic drop. Plot twist. Who is this adult woman birthing her control?

I am still very much a virgin airline, but I'm being presumptuous. I've decided that this summer it is going to happen: I will get pumped. And I need to go on the pill because I can't risk getting pregnant as I've got huge plans to go to Jamaica on my gap year and become a reggae tour manager.

'Helen, I would like to go on the pill.'

'Okay, Grace,' Helen said. 'So are you having sex?'

'No, I'm not having sex, Helen, but I will eventually one day very soon. So I think I should be safe, don't you, Helen?'

'I agree, it's important you are safe.' Helen had to ask me some admin questions before she could sign me off to go on the pill. When eventually she passed me a six-month supply of Microgynon, she said, 'Also, you must use condoms, Grace, with new sexual partners; the pill doesn't protect you from STDs. Okay?'

I nodded my head and made Helen think I was listening, but all I was thinking about was that I could finally say I was on the pill. I switched off when Helen started talking about STDs. Whenever an adult spoke about STDs I felt bored, like they were just using STDs to scare us into not having sex. A bit like when my mum told me that if I didn't floss my teeth I'd get gum disease when I'm old, and I was just like, how does this affect me? I'm a ripe young peach about to go on the pill. My gums are as fresh as Colgate's arsehole.

I was right, I did lose my virginity that summer, at last. And losing my virginity was weird. It reminded me a lot of the time when a straight man in the John Lewis underwear department measured my bra size. It was that level of uncomfortable.

The man I lost my virginity to, Freddie, was a mutual friend of my neighbour. I'd met Freddie at a dancehall night called Social Wednesdays in Oxford Street that we went to every week in our last year of school. I can tell you only one interesting thing about this scene when I had sex for the first time, and that was that Freddie smoked a spliff *throughout* our intercourse. I lost my virginity in a cloud of skunk. I was high, and I was bored. And even though I had a lifetime's supply of condoms under my bed, I didn't use one.

All that mattered was that I'd done it. And I didn't bleed, because I'm sure I'd already popped my cherry. Well, horse riding had popped my cherry – I'm sure I'd broken my hymen on a horse.

Isn't it funny that it's called a hymen? Like 'Hi, men! My hymen is broken, I'm not a virgin any more!'

•

I **realised that** the Brandon Centre was a much happier place for me before I started actually having sex. Going to a sexual-health clinic as a virgin is like going to a football match but not supporting a team: you've got nothing to lose. After my night with spliff-smoking Freddie, I started doing it a lot. I know you already know this, because you've had to hear it a lot. And I apologise to my parents, who have probably gone grey by now.

Actually, while I've got your attention and we're on apologies, Mum and Dad, I'm sure you'll be delighted to know that I always forgot to take my pill anyway. Soz! It was like moisturising for me. Some days I'd forget, some days I'd remember. My legs were flakey, and my unreliability with the pill meant that I took the morning-after pill like it was an iron supplement.

Have you had to get the morning-after pill before? It's a chore. Like descaling the kettle. Not that I've ever descaled a kettle, but it sounds like such a chore, doesn't it?

Let me paint you a picture of getting the morning-after pill. You go to a pharmacy – in certain pharmacies it's free, and in others you have to pay £35 for it.

You stand in a queue at the pharmacy with people picking up their prescriptions for their depression, diabetes or asthma. They look bored, and you're there panicking about the imminent moment you'll have to ask for the morning-after pill in front of all these people. You wish there was a code word like for Viagra, but you know if you try to be subtle, the pharmacist will make it even harder.

When you get to the front of the queue, you try to subtly whisper that you want the morning-after pill. 'Morning-after pill?' the pharmacist will say loudly. 'Wait there, and I will come and ask you a few questions.' The pharmacist wants to interview you. The pharmacist is literally walking around the counter to interview you. The pharmacist takes you off into a little side room. It's very hot in there, but at least you have privacy from the rest of the clientele.

Then the pharmacist asks you, 'How many times have you taken it in the last six months?'

'Hmm . . . ten?' you say.

'Ten?! That is a *lot*,' he says, because, of course, the pharmacist is a man. Sometimes he'll ask more intrusive questions, like the one who once asked me, 'Where did the sex take place?' To which I said, 'I can't remember,' to piss him off more.

Then he goes and gets the pill. He gives you the packet and makes you take it in front of him, as if he's your parent. He passes you one of those tiny pointy paper cups that look like they were meant for moulding spikey cakes with.

Before you leave, the pharmacist imparts some final words of wisdom. 'It's not a form of contraception, you know?' Is that a smirk on his face?

Of course you know that. But did he know that people of his gender also refuse to use condoms? That they never ask if you're on contraception or follow up to see if you've had their baby nine months later? Why aren't they here being shamed? You shuffle out of the pharmacy, still feeling grateful that you live in a world with that option available, despite the judgement you received in the process of it.

I always preferred going to the Brandon Centre rather than having to have one of these exchanges with a pharmacist who will never know what this feels like. I knew Helen would never shame me like that.

But the Brandon Centre was now starting to feel less novel. I noticed, in the waiting room, how many more girls there were than boys. Girls were taking responsibility for a situation that two people were creating, all because boys didn't care about our needs. How many times have you heard a dick owner say, 'Baaaaaaaabe, I just don't like using condoms, it doesn't feel as good,' then they make a pathetic sad face. 'It feels so nice being fully in you, pleaaaaaaaaase, baaaabe.' And you give in, because you think you have to, because you want to please them, because we're taught that we have to please men above all else.

Helen would tell me, every time, not to listen to my sexual partners when they tell me they hate wearing condoms. 'Grace, this isn't just about pregnancy, this is about STDs.' I understood that STDs were a thing, but still the only people I knew who had them were those two girls that fateful day at the Brandon Centre. They didn't scare me as much as the idea of getting pregnant ... or worse, rejected.

Rather than worrying about actually getting STDs, I was fuming about the fact that the burden of caring for our sexual health was left to girls, and not the owners of the penises that were sperming inside us, who were refusing to wear a condom. As my sexual self was coming alive, so was my burning dislike for all of the ways men had it easier than women. And sex would be no exception. Sexual health was another area of life which men could just walk and ejaculate through, with far fewer worries than women.

I wanted to get my own back. Once, while I was visiting Anna at Leeds University, I had a casual one-night stand with a friend of mine from school. I asked him not to come in me, but the little prick treated me like a sperm bank. Unfortunately, the next day was a Sunday, and the only place I could find the morning-after pill was a branch of Boots that was charging £35 for it. I had to pay £35 to undo the mistake of some boy. And so I wrote him an invoice. An invoice for £35. I delivered it personally to his halls, slipped it under his door and ran away. But do you think he paid for his sperm to be eradicated from my puss? Reader, he did not.

It was clear that men my age didn't really give a shit. But I did give a shit – just never in the moment. I obviously gave a shit because I went to the Brandon Centre more than I went to most of my best friend's houses. But I was still too willing to accept that my lovers didn't want to use condoms.

●

Luckily, I managed to avoid any major repercussions from intercourse before my gap year. For the first half of my gap year, I lived at home and worked as a waitress in three different restaurants, saving all of my money to go travelling. My parents also supported me during this time, but they thought my gap year was as ridiculous a concept as you probably do, so they said I could only go if I paid for it myself.

While all of my friends were going away together to South East Asia, I decided I wanted to go away alone, to the Caribbean. I wanted to improve my French in Guadeloupe (*bien sûr*, this was when I thought I was about to go and live in Paris for three years), and then I wanted to go to Jamaica to finally become Damian Marley's tour manager.

I had sex with two people during this four-month trip. In Guadeloupe I met a man called Cedric, who was from Paris. We had sex on the beach. We didn't have a condom. So I decided to use my not-so-trustworthy protection technique and ask him, '*Vous avez des diseases?*' He said no. Great. That must mean he's fine. Let's do it.

Same thing happened in Jamaica. I had sex with one person. A man called Kevin. We didn't use a condom.

'Do you have any STDs?'

'Course not,' he said. Sounds legit.

Guys, can I just say, this is not safe sex!!! Please listen to me. Asking someone if they have an STD and trusting their answer is like giving someone the keys to your house and asking them if they've ever burgled before.

When I was off in the Caribbean living my eighteen-year-old life, drinking rum at noon and going to the best dancehall nights I'd ever been to, STDs felt so far from my mind.

When I got back from my trip, one of the first things Anna did was make me get tested. She knew I was reckless with this stuff, and she had to gently nudge me to do it.

One really hot afternoon, Anna and I were sitting on Hampstead Heath and I got a call from an unknown number, which meant that it was probably bad news. 'Hi, Grace, we've got your results and we need you to come to the Royal Free Hospital as soon as possible.'

'What? Why? Can't I go to the Brandon Centre and see Helen?'

'Nope, we need you to come here.'

Anna and I rushed to the Royal Free Hospital – incidentally the hospital that I was born in. Now I was back for my rebirth. I was sweating profusely. We walked into the sexual-health building, which had its own secret entrance, I imagine because the rest of the hospital didn't want to be associated with people like me.

I felt lost as soon as we got in there. Every wall looked like it was crying out for decoration, but the boss of this secret sexual-health hospital wanted it to look as much like *Girl, Interrupted* as possible, so that we were traumatised when we came here and never wanted to come back.

It was so unlike the Brandon Centre. If the Brandon Centre was your local pub, this was a central-London Wetherspoons. Everyone who worked there looked miserable, as if there'd been a memo telling them to make this place as much like Hell or Starbucks as possible.

Anna and I were waiting on the rock-hard bench in silence – well, Anna was speaking but I couldn't tell you what about. A male doctor came into the waiting room who looked like the Child Catcher from *Chitty Chitty Bang Bang*. I hoped he wasn't going to call my name. Of course he did.

'Can I bring my friend in with me?' I asked the doctor.

'No.'

The doctor sat me down in his small, sinister doctor room. I planned my emergency exit, if I needed it, but then I realised that the only exit in the room was the door. God, Grace, you're so basic. He was very thin, with a pointy face and thick glasses. He looked like he hated me already. I wished I was with Helen. I'd forgotten his name by now and started having intrusive thoughts about accidentally calling him the Child Catcher while we were mid-conversation.

'So, Grace, you have gonorrhea.' I definitely heard that and I started to cry instantly. I knew this was bad. But I didn't know much else. I'd heard of gonorrhea in the same way that I'd heard in London you're never further than eight feet from a rat. But I'd still never seen one.

I didn't know the specifics of gonorrhea – where does it live? How does it form? What happens when you have it? The fact that I'd been dragged in there to meet Mr Pointy Child Catcher made me feel like I was going to be fatally ill. Surely if it was curable, they'd have just texted me? I'm dying. Fuck. I cried even harder.

'You don't need to cry,' he said. I hate this man. I want to set a herd of cattle on his pointy face. 'It's treatable.'

I stop crying, which relieves him. I still don't say anything, which probably relieves him even more.

'We just wanted you to come in here because it's a bit of a rare disease. Have you been travelling recently?'

'Yes.'

'Where?'

'The Caribbean.'

'Right. Well, HIV is very prevalent there.'

'Okay, but I don't have HIV, do I?'

He gets angry. As in, I can visibly see the rage rising out of his shirt collar in a red rash. 'Well, Grace . . . you had unprotected sex in the Caribbean!'

'Yes, I did.'

'And it's quite stupid to have unprotected sex in the Caribbean, isn't it? Don't you know that?'

I knew this guy was a prick. I did not have a global picture on unsafe-sex hotspots.

'I didn't know there was HIV there.'

He looks deeply unimpressed. 'When did you last have sex?'

'Two weeks ago.'

'Well, the HIV won't show up in your blood for two months after the intercourse, so you'll have to come and do a test in six weeks.' And with that he turned to his computer to book in the appointment.

Before I left, the Child Catcher told me not to have sex with anyone in this time. 'I won't be having sex ever again,' I said. He looked delighted.

'This really isn't that bad, Grace,' said Anna when we left the hospital. 'You're not gonna have it, I swear.' I started crying again.

'Six weeks?! I have to wait six weeks to find out. That's basically two months!'

'It'll fly by,' Anna said – that's such an Anna thing to say, as if the next six weeks were going to be fun.

'I'm such a fucking moron. Why didn't I read the leaflets in the Brandon Centre?'

'Listen, you're gonna be fine! And maybe this happened because you needed to learn from it. You've been too reckless.'

I got home and pretended to my mum that everything was fine. I went to my bedroom and called Tyler, saying, 'I have some bad news ... I might have HIV, but I won't know for six months.'

'Are you sure it's not six weeks?' Tyler asks. 'I've just spoken to Anna and she said it was six weeks.'

I watched the episode of *The OC* when Seth kisses Summer in the Spiderman mask, and I cried for my stupid self. I knew HIV was really treatable now, but I couldn't stop thinking about how this whole situation could have been completely avoided.

•

For all of those six weeks, I was an energy vampire. I enjoyed nothing, and I wanted to make sure none of my friends around me could enjoy anything either. I was depressed. Every party we'd go to, we'd have to leave because I was hysterically crying in the toilet. The girls kept buying me Maltesers, knowing Maltesers were one of the only things that could always make me happy. But even Maltesers tasted like Jacob's crackers with no butter on.

When the six weeks were up I took the test, and I didn't have it. And by that point the gonorrhea had been treated. I was given a clean bill of sexual health again, and to celebrate the relief I felt, I got incredibly, fantastically drunk. And I never had unprotected sex again. That's not true. Imagine if I'd really learnt a lesson so easily! But I was a lot safer, and I also started being really firm with the men I slept with. Asking the right questions, having the hard conversations, insisting on safe sex.

At the Brandon Centre, I had learnt so much about what support there is to avoid pregnancy and STDs. Helen had given us the cold, hard facts, and without her I would have been completely lost. But what we didn't learn were the less scientific facts around sex. How to insist on using a condom with your partner. How important it is to have a conversation with your partner about STDs. That STDs are just diseases that you catch, but you have to treat them with care because they can affect your fertility.

Since gonorrhea gate, I started learning more and more about sex. About how bodies work, and what they can do. I've learnt most of these things from experience, and to be honest, most of them I wish I'd learnt sooner. So, here are the rest of my takeaways about sex. Some of them are about shame, some of them are about safety, some of them are about sensational sex, and some are just random things I think you should know.

WHAT I WISH I HAD BEEN TAUGHT AT SCHOOL ABOUT SEX

Fanny farts don't smell

Listen to me, you should never, in your whole wide long life, be ashamed of fanny farting. I wish that someone had mentioned to me that when you have sex, sometimes you will fanny fart. Fanny farting is so casual. They do not smell. It's basically when a bit of air gets trapped in your fanny, and it wants to get out, and as it does it makes a noise. They are literally air that your fanny has breathed in and is now breathing out. Don't be embarrassed, ever. The next time you fanny fart when you're having sex, if you feel embarrassed, just say that your vagina is playing the bagpipes right now, and move on.

Don't put a Malteser up your vagina

Don't put anything random up your vagina. Companies like to sell us all of this shit like femfresh and fanny deodorant, but our pH level is a sensitive princess. You shouldn't put anything up there that isn't water-based, ever. Nothing sugary, even if it is to prove that you can fanny fart a Malteser out and into your boyfriend's mouth – don't do it. When I did that, I got thrush for three weeks. I couldn't sit down without rubbing and itching. Be kind to your vagina. It smells wonderful already, so don't fuck with that.

Foreplay is moreplay

When you start having sex, it's always a rush to get to the end of the race, and usually I'd be the loser. Contrary to common teenage perception, you won't come immediately if stuff is just being shoved inside you like a sardine. You need to build up the vibes with foreplay. Foreplay is like the pre-drinks of sex. The pre-drinks happen before the party and help get you hyped up. Don't forget the pre-drinks, because they're the build-up to something very exciting.

Trans men are men and trans women are women

I don't know who you are reading this. I don't know what your opinions are on trans rights, and the existence of trans people, and I hope you're already educated enough to understand this, but I'm going to say it anyway because transphobia is terrifyingly present in society right now, and it's so important that we are allies to trans people at all costs. I am going to state it very simply: trans men are men, and trans women are women. Cis people do not get to decide somebody else's gender identification. That isn't in their power. They also can't begin to understand what it is like to grow up in a body you don't feel at home in, because you've been born into the wrong gender.

And listen to trans people. As my amazing friend, the trans-activist and model Munroe Bergdorf, says, 'If you want to know what is best for trans people, listen to trans people. More specifically, black trans women who are navigating racism and transphobia. Listen to the supportive parents of trans kids who have watched their children flourish after being listened to.'

Tell your partner when you haven't come

Have you heard of the pleasure gap? You know about the pay gap, right? Men getting paid more than women for the same job, and even worse, white people getting paid more than BIPOC for the same job.

Okay, so the pleasure gap is the same but for pleasure and orgasms. An American study found that straight women orgasm less than any other demographic. In a heterosexual couple, men are four times more likely to come than women are. This is no surprise because when straight men are involved, they think women come from a single pump, and they just come and forget about you.

Straight men and gay men are the most likely demographics to orgasm. Lesbians and bisexual women fall behind those, and straight women come last. I fear we've allowed straight men for far too long to get away with not prioritising our pleasure. In lying to your partners about coming, you're feeding into the pleasure gap. DON'T DO IT. They need to know they didn't make you come, and then they'll try to do it next time, and if they don't, put them in the Dickheads Anonymous bin.

Sex on your period is lit

We're already taught that our periods are a grim and unwelcome element of our bodies, and on top of that, when they're happening we're supposedly not allowed to have sex. Fuck that to the moon and back. Don't let yourself be shamed into thinking you can't have sex when you're bleeding. You can. Put a towel down on the bed and then carry on as usual. And again, if people shame you about your period, put them in the Dickheads Anonymous bin.

Don't swallow cum on an empty stomach

That stuff is like a shot of sambuca and I'm telling you, if you haven't eaten for a long time, you won't keep it in.

Wear a fucking condom

I hope you didn't miss the bit earlier when I told you about the time I recklessly got an STD and how stupid I was for not using protection. I only told that story so that you WON'T MAKE THAT SAME MISTAKE. So please, if someone tells you you're lame for wanting to use protection, tell them they're a super-spreader and that they need to pluck their eyebrows.

When it comes to your sexuality, there's always someone to talk to

I am straight, so I can't speak from personal experience on the process of coming out, but I do know from having Jack in my life for so long that for anyone in the LGBTQ+ community, growing up can be isolating. And this can obviously have a huge effect on your mental health. And then there's the trauma of being exposed to so much homophobia and abuse as a result of your identity. What's amazing about the world today is that, thanks to the gorgeous Internet, there is a community for whatever you're going through. If you are feeling isolated by your experiences, whether you're gay, queer, trans or anything else, there will be people online you can talk to and communities you can become part of. Also, you'll be surprised by how open people in your life are to talking about it, and if they're not, social media is full of amazing communities that will help you feel less alone. See Goddess Platform, the Brook charity and Exist Loudly.

Do to your pubes as they would be done by

For so much of my life, I've felt confused about what to do with my pubes. I was told endlessly at school that we must have hairless vaginas. But I couldn't work out what I actually wanted. For a while I waxed them all off, but then I panicked that I only wanted them waxed because I'd been told I needed a hairless vagina. But then, having no hair made me feel like I had a baby's vagina. And I didn't understand why people wanted a child's vagina. I was on a loop in my head: which came first? The desire for a hairless vagina, or the knowledge that a hairless vagina was what I was supposed to have?

However, I've never met a sexual partner who's minded my vagina being hairy or hairless. Sure, boys learn from porn that girls are supposed to be hairless, but in my experience, when someone is being granted the sex, they're happy about that. And if he does say something about your pubes, he's an absolute clown, so again, put him in the Dickheads Anonymous bin.

So what I want to say on pubes is that you shouldn't do something because other people are telling you to do it; you should do the thing that you want to do in that moment. It's like with food; we don't let other people tell us what food to eat. We don't eat the same food all of our lives; we eat what we feel like eating in that moment. Same for pubes. You don't have to commit to one style; just do what you're feeling at that time. Sometimes Scary Spice, sometimes Baby Spice and sometimes, in my case, Ginger Spice.

Don't eat Kellogg's

Have you heard of Kellogg's? You know, the cereal empire Kellogg's? Coco Pops, Cheerios, Corn Flakes. Well, I've got a story for you about Corn Flakes, one of Kellogg's' first cereals. The person who started Kellogg's was a doctor. His name? Doctor John Harvey Kellogg. He was a doctor, but also a leading figure in the anti-masturbation movement. This was a movement of doctors in the late 1800s and early 1900s who believed that masturbation was a terrible crime and that if women wanked they would end up with all kinds of illnesses. Illnesses like uterine cancer, epilepsy, depression and, my personal favourite, bad posture. Dr Kellogg believed that wanking could do all of that to a woman.

What's more, Dr Kellogg believed that sugary foods made people want to wank, so he wanted to create a cereal that was so bland it would stop people from wanking. And so he created Corn Flakes. The blandest cereal of them all. The cereal that needs to be topped by a spoonful of sugar for it to be edible. Corn Flakes were made to stop women from wanking. I was more of a Coco Pops girl any way so . . .

Girls wank, too

Now, as you know, I had my first wank when I was seven years old. I wanked probably once a week after that until I was thirteen. After that, I upped the ante. I was wanking twice, maybe three times a week. It was a short-term hit. When it was happening, it felt like my vagina was on a cloud. But the long-term effect was that I hated myself so much, because I truly thought I was a freak. I remember once at school, my friends and I were hanging out in the back field, in a circle. Anna mentioned that someone we knew, called Maya, wanked.

'Ewwwwww, that's so fucking gross,' everyone said in unison, me included.

I wish I'd just said, 'Yeah, me too, so what?' Because now I know that some of them were also doing it, and we were all hiding it from each other. That could have been an amazing moment, when we all came out as wankers. But we didn't feel we could, and I spent years after that hating my wanking self.

Then one day, when I was eighteen, I met this older girl called Harriet at a wedding. Harriet was twenty-three, which felt like years above me, plus she'd already had loads of boyfriends and sex with a lot of people. Harriet took me under her wing. We went outside for a cigarette and she asked me if I had ever wanked. Oh fuck, this is my chance to admit it.

'Yeah, I do,' I said, terrified.

'Me too. I started humping things when I was a kid and I've wanked ever since.' And just like that, I sighed away the shame that I'd been carrying for eleven years. Finally, I knew that girls wank, too.

NEVER HAD A WANK BEFORE? FOLLOW THESE SIMPLE INSTRUCTIONS:

1) Order a vibrator. Maybe some lube, too.

2) When the vibrator arrives, clean it.

3) Get into bed and set some mood lighting if you can.

4) Put on a sexy piece of material. Some feminist, ethical porn. Erika Lust is my favourite.

5) Don't feel you need to be turned on straight away. Be patient, watch the material for a bit with the vibrator exploring around your clit.

6) If you don't come the first time, don't worry. No time spent wanking is wasted; it's all part of the journey towards learning how to give yourself pleasure. Keep going. I believe in you.

LOOKING MY VAGINA IN THE EYE

If you've made it to this point in the book, congratulations. I hope you've been able to connect with me. As I told you at the beginning, I care A LOT about what people think of me.

One thing that's been on my mind is that what you might take from me so far is that I was ashamed of being single, and that I have a negative attitude about the single life. I mean, from rejection, to rape, to STDs, my portrayal so far has been the grim without the gorgeous.

But it was sometimes Samantha Jones-level fun. And, for me, shame has never been tied up in not having a boyfriend. Sometimes being single means you're exposed to the things that can cause shame (see previous chapters), but it also means you can have ridiculous amounts of fun. Wild and weird and unexpected fun, which can turn into amazing stories for stand-up.

Like this one ... a brief snippet of totally shameless behaviour, just for you.

Not long after I'd started doing stand-up, I was randomly asked to do a set at a women's health summit in Turkey. This was no ordinary summit. It was a summit organised by supermodel and superhuman Natalia Vodianova. Everyone attending this health summit was either rich or a model, or both.

It was at the most incredible resort in Antalya I've ever been to in my life. This was no Butlin's. Every room, every pool, every restaurant looked like the Kardashians were about to enter with their film crew, to sit down for a little spot of salad. If only.

I'd been asked to go to the event to do a funny feminist 'speech' about 'women's health'. That was my only brief. You guys know me by now, and I'm sure you won't be surprised to hear that I decided to write my set about wanking. Wanking? Of course, *j'adore*. I was twenty-four at this point and very obsessed with talking about wanking. That's so in the past – not at all wanking-obsessed now. Not at all.

When I arrived at the resort, I met the man who had booked me. Paul, his name was. Paul was quite sunburnt, which made me relate to him a lot in a sea of supermodels. 'We're so excited to have you here,' Paul said. 'You're on stage at midday.'

'Great. Just thought I should let you know, my set is about wanking. That's cool, right?' Paul's face went a brighter shade of red.

'Oh no, Grace! You can't do a set about wanking!' he shispered (this is a shout/whisper, a very potent form of communication). 'The First Lady of Turkey is here . . . and this is a Muslim country. If you talk about wanking, you'll be in trouble.'

Fuck. I wrote a whole set about wanking. Do I have any material that isn't about wanking or Tony Blair?

Looking my vagina in the eye

'Absolutely fair enough,' I told him. 'Let me go and re-write it.' I had an hour before I was due to go on stage and perform to a room full of the most beautiful people in the world. I had an hour to write something that would spark joy in them. That would make them laugh. That would make them remember me. What I wrote wasn't really a comedy set. I don't know what it was. But I kind of think it's magic.

Hello,

I'm very happy to be here. This is the fanciest hotel I've ever stayed in. Being rich really pays off, doesn't it? Congratulations, guys.

I am a comedian and an activist. Most of the material I'm working on at the moment is about British politics, which is a vibe kill, honestly . . . or sex, but I know it's a bit early for that. So for today I've written something for you that is sort of comedy, sort of not comedy. It's a piece called 'Looking My Vagina in the Eye'. By the way, I know I'm supposed to call her a vulva, but I've been calling her my vagina for so long that I'm just going to do it now. Please do laugh if you find it funny, because otherwise I'll feel very insecure.

For the first nineteen years of my life I managed to never, ever, ever, ever make eye contact with my vagina. I knew it was there, obviously; I'd clean it, occasionally, and I'd stuff tampons up it once a month to stop blood from pouring onto my Juicy Couture tracksuit.

But I'd never dare look it in the eye. If my vagina ever tried to look me in the eye, I'd be like 'No, [covers eyes] don't look at me, bruv!'

My vagina was like a broken mirror. If I looked directly into it, I'd be cursed with bad sex for the rest of my life. What I hadn't realised was that I'd actually be cursed with bad sex anyway, whether I made eye contact with my vagina or not, because teenage boys don't know how to fuck.

My vagina and I have always had a turbulent relationship. When I was seven years old I masturbated for the first time. But this was a mentally expensive wank. Afterwards, I loathed myself. I thought I was so fucked up I'd be arrested.

At thirteen, a boy at the school next to mine told me 'all vaginas smell like fish'. And so, out of a fear of smelling like fish, I set off on a journey to find the best products to make my vagina sparkly, like a unicorn bath bomb. But I ended up just getting chronic thrush. Who knew that was a thing? ME NOW.

At fourteen my periods started and then, once a month, my vagina felt like it was under attack from the enemy. This period blood wasn't the blue blood the ads had shown me, and there certainly wasn't just a droplet of it. My vagina made my pants look like a fight scene in a Tarantino movie. My hatred for it grew.

Looking my vagina in the eye

At sixteen, a different boy told me that men would never have sex with a girl if she had pubes. He said, 'Women with hair on their vaginas end up alone and cold.' I still, to this day, have no idea what he meant by that, because surely one thing hair is good for is warmth? But from that day on, the hair had to go. I shaved my pubes till there was just skin, and then I shaved the skin off like Parmesan gratings on a spag bol. My vagina looked like it had chicken pox.

When I was eighteen, I had sex for the first time. Finally, all those years of masturbating had actually led to something real and grown up. But this boy didn't understand my vagina at all. He was looking right at it – which was more than I'd ever done – but it was like my grandma trying to negotiate the world of Netflix. I pretended to come. Oohs and aaaahs and FUCKs and *Insert loud shrieking moans seen in unrealistic pornography*. But all I was thinking was, 'I could do this so much better myself.'

When I was nineteen, something really bad happened. Really bad.

I fanny farted. I didn't even know fanny farts were a thing! I fanny farted so loud during sex that the boy leaped out of my vagina and shouted, 'There's something wrong with you!' The next day I went to the doctor's because I was sure fanny farts were a symptom of cancer. I went to the doctor. I sat down in her chair: 'I have something very wrong with my vagina.'

'What happened?' the doctor said. She was used to me coming in by now.

'I farted . . . out of my vagina.'

'Grace, you come here too often with these issues . . . You have nothing wrong with you.'

'I do. My vagina is sick.'

'Go home and look at your vagina in the mirror. There is nothing wrong with it.'

I went home. I put my vagina up against the mirror. I looked her directly in the eye. After nineteen years. And when I looked her in the eye, this sweet, gorgeous girl who's been supporting me my whole life, I fell in love. She was absolutely gorgeous. If only she could have her own Instagram account. She'd be an influencer.

As women, we're conditioned by society to bully and attack our vaginas. The internalised hatred that I have for my pubes, my periods, my camel-toe, my fanny farting is so deep-rooted and hard to unpick that just thinking about it makes me want to fall into a deep nap and fart throughout.

The patriarchy doesn't want women to be proud of their vaginas, and all of the amazing things we can do with them. Because once our vaginas are self-sufficient, the patriarchy won't have the power to control and commodify them, and they hate that, because once we realise we can come without men, I mean, really, what's the point of them?

I advise you all to go back to your rooms after this, go to a mirror and look your vagina in the eye. Look at it for so long, and then I promise you, you will, too, fall in love. And then, once you've fallen in love with your vagina, people will fall in love with you. But most importantly, you'll be so in love with yourself you won't need anyone else.

[STANDING OVATION]

And reader, I advise you to do the same. Go on, quickly. Pause this for a monumental moment, get a mirror and look your vagina in the eye. And don't you dare tell me you're not in love.

And this, my lovers, is a true story of a self-love-fulfilling prophecy. After I delivered this weird speech that I wrote in an hour, I was the talk of the event. Me talking about being in love with my vagina made people want to talk to me. It was like secondary school all over again.

I decided I should try to shag someone. I had an amazing luxury suite with two bedrooms and a hot tub – what else can you do with that space? I should bang someone. There was a closing party that night, because these rich models treated the women's summit like it was a season in Ibiza. The party took place at a club, which was on a cliff hanging over the sea. That night, I was the nearest to being famous I'll probably ever feel in my life. People were queuing up to tell me how much they loved my speech and how much it had helped them – or would help other women they knew – love their vaginas.

Then a guy came up to me. 'I loved your speech,' he said in a sultry Turkish accent. He was a photographer – can't remember his name, but he told me I was his favourite part of the event. Of course I was. I'm in love with my vagina. And of course he wanted to have sex with me. When we got back to my two-bedroom suite with a jacuzzi, we were in bed and the photographer was going down on me, giving me head. When he looked up at me, with my fanny juice on his face, he said: 'I'm looking your vagina in the eye – and I love it.'

DON'T WORK WITH
MEN UNLESS YOU
HAVE TO

After I left university in Paris. I decided to change my direction. Academia, it was clear, was never going to be for me. Nor was, after a certain exchange with Tupperware, a campus university. Leo was at an art school in South London doing a really practical film-making degree. He persuaded me to apply, and I got in. It was the perfect medium, I could still live my life in London with my same friends, while getting a degree.

On my first day at art school, I wore a baby-blue velour tracksuit with a brand-new pair of Air Force 1s. I looked like a Powerpuff Girl who'd got addicted to drugs and left the puff gang to sell poppers in Camden Market instead. I sat down in the lecture room, and as soon as I looked at the other students I realised something major. This is crazy – you're really not gonna believe this, guys – but I realised . . . for the first time in my life, I wasn't going to be in the popular group. Not in this baby-blue velour tracksuit. No, babes.

I'd always been popular. I was loud and alpha and was good at making friends, and you probably think I sound like a dickhead by now anyway so I'm not gonna lie about my stellar popularity record. But at art school, I was like the egg that the sperm rejected.

I've always loathed art people. Not art itself – I love art, I am a work of art. I'm not joking. Above my bed I have a nude painting of myself that someone did when I modelled at a life-drawing class. If you saw it, you'd probably think it was by Matisse. See, I know art. An aside, but why are all paintings called 'Oil on canvas'?

It's not the actual art I dislike, it's art people. The type of people who say things like, 'I only dress in charity-shop clothes, sorry, I've never heard of Urban Outfitters, but that's just me!' as if they invented second-hand clothes.

I find art people can make bullshitting an art form in itself. And art school was full of people who loved to talk shit about art. Another shock. It was full of people who could collectively orgasm over a painting of a square. People who would talk about their own art as being part of a non-existent revolution against capitalism. These were people who could talk about narratives and metanarratives while they were getting drunk in a pub.

They loved to talk about nothing, while making you feel intellectually inferior for not speaking nothingness with them. My course was like a shit-chatting Olympics. Every day there was a new person trying to get that gold medal by talking for forty-five minutes about the symbolism of the moon. These were people who were desperate to show off the fact that they'd seen all of Jean-Luc Godard's movies. It's, like, no big deal; I've seen Jean-Luc Godard's films, too, without subtitles, *j'adore*, but I've also seen every episode of *Sex and the City* ten times and I think that's just as good. I'm not vacuous for thinking so.

In the first term I developed a huge crush on a boy called Alfie, the lead bullshitter. Alfie was tall but looked very young. He had very doughy, smooth skin that looked like pitta bread. He had massive eyes that made him look like he was high all the time. He was handsome in a geeky Silicon Valley kind of way. He dressed like a laid-back dad from the Cotswolds, in unbranded trainers and khaki trousers. Both things that would usually never be acceptable to me. But Alfie was the star of the course. I think he'd been studying cinema for longer than he'd been wanking, and it showed. He had a scent about him – ambition mixed with a total lack of self-awareness. Like Timothée Chalamet in *Call Me by Your Name*. Of course I fancied him. You would have, too.

Alfie used to ask me to go outside and stand with him while he smoked roll-ups on the roundabout of Elephant and Castle. It was always impossible to light a roll-up on this roundabout, because it's the epicentre of the world's wind. Much like my vagina.

But I'd go and watch him relight his cigarette every few seconds. He'd ask me what films I liked. *Mean Girls* was still my favourite, but I couldn't say that to him, because I knew he would call me vapid. So I would lie and tell him about my obsession with Wes Anderson. Then he would start talking about films by a filmmaker I didn't know, and I'd wish I'd just said *Mean Girls*.

Then, in the second term, Alfie and I got to work together. This was it – we're gonna fall in love while making a film together and become a dynamic film-making duo, I thought. My dad won't approve of him because he's too posh and not remotely interested in football, but that's absolutely fine, because we'll live in our own creative bubble, like Greta Gerwig and Noah Baumbach.

But very quickly I realised my dreams of working with Alfie would be like Luton Airport; unglamorous and chaotic. Alfie was more than a flawed artist; he was a terrible one. He knew all about film in theory, but nothing about how to actually make a film. He was like a kid at Legoland who thought that because he'd got a driving licence there, he could drive a Land Rover in the real world.

Alfie and I clashed on pretty much everything. Not in a 'sexual tension, might fuck it out' way. By the time I'd heard more than three of his suggestions for 'lingering black-and-white shots of the back of a man's head to display distortion' (I mean, what the fuck??), his appeal had dwindled to a flat nothing. But Alfie *had* to be the one who came up with all of the ideas. He *had* to get the credit. He hated it when someone else had a good idea, and when they did, he would reject it and come back five minutes later with that same idea repackaged, claiming it as his own. He was like a football player who would berate his teammates for scoring a goal, because if it wasn't him that scored it, it was a loss. In my beautiful, sapphic, supportive Parli Hill bubble, I'd literally never encountered a man in my creative or intellectual space. At school it was like we fought to give each other credit and build each other up. I'd never seen anything like this – and, oh boy, was it a shock.

Over the time we worked together I went from thinking maybe he was right, to knowing he was wrong and trying to challenge him, to just giving up and letting it slide. Sound familiar? Sound like every time you've had to work with a man? At the time I thought it was just Alfie.

Then, one day after filming, Alfie and I are in the student bar, which is, of course, called the Dark Room Bar, because we are artistes, and our bar has to be named after the dark rooms that photos are processed in. It's only 2 p.m., but the room has no natural light, as its really sticking to the theme, so it feels like night-time. We are both drinking gin and tonics, although Alfie is drinking slimline tonic, which makes me feel weird, but I can't explain why.

I've realised recently that Alfie doesn't really ask me any questions about myself – another pattern I'm getting too comfy with. So I'm listening to him talk shit about his housemates in Peckham who won't let him have a house party on his birthday. I'm really bored, and I'm downing my drink as fast as I can just so I can go to the bar for another one and escape this brutally inconvenient conversation.

I try to change the subject. 'Do you fancy any of the girls on the course?' I ask, now that my crush on him has been buried in Highgate Cemetery next to Karl Marx's tomb.

'Nahh, not really.' He bites his nail. 'I don't think there are many talented girls on our course.' That's not what I asked him, but he sees talent and sex appeal as the same thing. I know this should be a good thing. Like, wow, that rare beast: a man who's not solely interested in how fit a girl is. But firstly, I don't believe him. And secondly, how has he managed to make talent a commodity of male approval. Like, 'Mmmm, Georgia O'Keeffe is an unparalleled painter of vision and depth, don't you just want to fuck her?'

'Sorry, but that's bullshit,' I say. 'There are so many girls who are insanely talented on our course.' I start listing off their names. He laughs a tiny little unsatisfying laugh.

'I just don't think women are good at concentrating on stuff.'

Now I'm raging. 'Sorry . . . what? You don't think I can concentrate on things?'

He panics and says, 'No, no, not you. Just, like, loads of them – they're too preoccupied with looking good.'

What was wild to me about this comment was that Alfie was impossible to work with because he was completely, totally focused on what other people thought of him. All he cared about was that everyone else thought he was the daredevil, the next Tarantino, the tortured artist who will storm the planet with a film that changes mankind's perception of . . . mankind.

'It's funny you say that,' I say, 'because that's actually what people have been saying about you.' It's nice to see pure panic in a dickhead's eyes sometimes.

Alfie was a basic, unimaginative, undrained tea towel parading as an artiste. Alfie didn't like the fact that girls could be gorgeous and talented. He was shaking in his unbranded trainers at the fact that women had more interesting life perspectives to make films about. And he hated that we could actually concentrate on something for longer than an Instagram story.

I hoped this wasn't an all-men thing, and just an Alfie thing, but unfortunately I was starting to see how many men were coming out as dummy-sucking babies. I started clashing with one of my teachers, a middle-aged man called Horatio. Horatio was a smart but slightly failed film-maker. I mean, with a name like that, surely his parents knew they were setting him up to fail? It's like they wanted to ensure that their son would end up a complete twat. Horatio was desperate to prove to a bunch of undergrad roll-up smokers that he was an incredible film-maker, the best film-maker ever to exist in the movie-making world. He had to use every moment as a way of showing us that he knew more about films than we did, because, in his self-serving words, he'd actually 'been in the business'. But it was obvious he'd not succeeded there, because those who can't do teach, and those who can't teach get into fights with me.

Horatio and I fought a lot, because I didn't like that he was on a constant mission to patronise and mansplain his deficient knowledge of film-making to us. He wanted to dictate what our personal styles should be, and I thought that was ridiculous.

So I got good at passive-aggressively putting my hand up and saying, 'Horatio, you're wrong.' Horatio hated it when I suggested he wasn't the wise old sage he thought he was. A passive-aggressive comment in return would quickly morph into him doing a very good impersonation of me when I was five and my parents had told me I couldn't have another scoop of mint-choc-chip ice cream.

I was used to dealing with alpha men with egos, because, well, my dad. My dad had shown me what a confident man looks like, and he'd also explained what an insecure man with an ego looks like (*cough*, Toothy T, *cough*). I'd seen these men in suits in politics so many times, but honestly, I was a bit shocked to see that they existed in the art world, too. I looked from Horatio to Alfie and thought, 'Fuck, are these ego-driven, desperately insecure men going to repeatedly show up in my working life as well as my personal life? Do we need to make a law saying that they need to be educated for longer so they can grow out of this shit?'

Do the boys who don't think girls have talent become the men who mock and minimise girls they're threatened by?

Because, really, there was no difference between men like Alfie and Horatio. Apart from thirty years and sex appeal, they were exactly the same. In this world, the Alfies turn into the Horatios. Mediocre men continue to pretend they're the talented ones while the women are second-guessing themselves. I was sort of relieved when I made this connection, because I realised it wasn't me. It wasn't that I was a terrible artist and Alfie had to teach me the ways. It was that some men (not all men, blah blah) don't want you to be talented, because it throws their lack of talent into relief. I knew I was being fooled here, but I hadn't quite realised how difficult working with men was going to be.

•

I was really lucky starting out, because, well, nepotism. Nepotism is a very real thing and I benefited from it a lot. I knew people in the film and TV industry through my family, and my dad being who he was helped me get my foot into doors. I'm not proud of this, but at the time I didn't see how lucky I was to have that head start.

I think it's important to be accountable for nepotism. I know a lot of people who will pretend that they started their career themselves or got to the top through 'hard work', and obviously you *do* need to work hard, but these people want you to think they did it all themselves, when they didn't. I don't like that, because they're essentially gaslighting other people into thinking they are better than them. I think the most important thing is that, if you benefit from nepotism, you should also bring people in with you – people who might not have access to these same nepotistic avenues.

I started off having meetings with different people in TV, pitching ideas and usually getting rejected or being told to come back when the idea was a little more 'formed'. I noticed something in these rooms: that whenever I was in a meeting with a man, they would never look at me. Even when they addressed me, they'd look at a wall or, even more kindly, at the other man in the room.

I was basically like the bin in the room. I had a purpose, but these men didn't want to look at me while I was being used.

I didn't mention this to anyone because I just presumed it was because I was a young woman with breasts, and my idea of men was so basic that I presumed they felt nervous. I was so painfully desperate for success that I didn't want to talk about things that seemed trivial, because I thought it would make me seem difficult, and I knew that I was so lucky to even be there in the first place, I don't want to test things.

I didn't want to be difficult then, when I was twenty-one, I just wanted to be a success. I wanted to be like all the people I'd grown up around, like all the people I'd watched on TV. I wanted to be a rich man and a powerful

woman. I wanted to be a fashionable, cool, sexually liberated party girl, who was also a business bitch who was
listed in *Forbes* 30 under 30, and I would do anything I
could to achieve that.

I decided to write my first feature film, which was called
Sweetie. The script was a comedy drama (*j'adore*) about a
grey-area rape (*je déteste*) that was, as you can imagine,
inspired by my own experiences. The film's main premise
was that it was about a young woman who was a bit of a
wreckhead. When she gets raped by her friend from work,
she moves back home with her mum, just when her
grandma has moved back in with dementia. It was a script
about women, and sexual assault, and I'd written it about
a year before #metoo properly broke.

This script helped me get a writing agent, and then my
agents sent the script around to loads of production
companies, some of whom were taking an interest in it. I
started going for loads of meetings – or, as Tyler and I call
them, 'mittings', because we like making something grown
up sound like it's for children. So production companies
were liking my script and wanting to take mittings with
my twenty-one-year-old self.

In the meantime, I was very lucky to be making a prank
show called *Riot Girls,* to mark 100 years since (some)
women's suffrage. I had worked closely with a production
company developing this, and I was writing, producing
and performing in it. It was me and three other comedians

– Sophie Duker, Cam Spence and Jen Wakefield – pranking men about very important issues like period taboo, the gender pay gap, manspreading and the world's obsession with pubes.

So while I was in the pre-production phase of *Riot Girls*, I'd been invited to a mitting at a very prestigious production company based in Camden to discuss my feature-film script. I won't say their name for *legal reasons*, but they had read *Sweetie*, and were interested in meeting with me to discuss developing it into a TV show.

I was so excited for this mitting that I had a nervous wank before I started getting ready. They were a big production company and I thought I'd walk in that door, they'd fall in love with me, because who wouldn't? And *voilà*, *j'adore*, Grace Campbell is the new hot thing – like vaping.

I got dressed up for the mitting. I liked to dress up for these mittings with production companies in a distinctively Grace style. I never wanted people to think I'd dressed up formally for them. This was very important in establishing that I didn't care what people thought of me. So I wore a baggy pair of camouflage army trousers that I'd bought in an army shop in Paris, and a red silk jacket with loads of gold chains. I looked like a hoot.

I arrived outside the production company's offices early. From the outside I could see that they were swanky verging on wanky. I told the receptionist who I was meeting and she said, 'Great, if you'd like to take a seat, they'll be out in a minute.' I didn't know anything about who I was meeting. My agents had told me I was meeting two men, but that was all I knew. I didn't know if they were straight men or not. Since uni, I had only worked with gay men in the industry. I felt safe with LGBTQ+ people, and I hope they felt safe with me. With them and women I always felt that I could connect over our collective hatred of the patriarchy. And especially so when I am talking about sexual trauma. No one wants to talk about that with a straight twat.

So I'm waiting in the swanky reception, scrolling through Instagram thinking about what my next post should be – maybe this picture of me and Anna on the heath. What shall I have for lunch today? I calculate where the nearest Pret is and how long it would take me to get there before I have to get on the Tube for my next mitting.

Two men walk into the reception. They're both white and their faces are boringly decorated. They were both dressed in streetwear, which means clothes that sixteen-year-olds were wearing and selling on Depop. The older one was bald, and he had a smug face which made me think he wasn't going to like me. The other guy was younger; he looked like he wasn't much older than me.

I could tell from his face that the bald one was disappointed by how I looked. I had a feeling he was the type of man that never likes women like me. I call them the posh unilads. The types of guys who went to boarding school, but when they were there they thought they were too hard for it, even though their parents own an estate in Scotland where they hunt deer for 'fun'. The types of guys who will do anything for other men to rate them but think women like me have no purpose.

'Hi, I'm Matt,' the bald one says. 'Nice to meet you, errr . . . mate.'

He has forgotten my name, and he feels I'm not attractive enough to call 'babe'.

'I'm Grace.'

'I'm Nick,' the other one says.

'Did you come in from far away? Bit of a random spot this,' Matt says. Is he saying Camden is random? It's in Zone One.

'No, I live round the corner.'

'Lucky you,' says Nick.

'Yeah, it is lucky,' I say.

They both laugh, which feels like a slight.

'We're super-excited to meet you,' Matt says, as we sit down in a pod in the café area of the building. 'We loved *Sweetie*.'

'Thanks. I'm pretty proud of it, too.'

'How long did it take you to write it?' Nick asks.

'Like a week,' I say. 'It just came out quickly.'

'Was it based on your experiences?' Matt asks. I can't work out if he is genuinely interested, but I feel like I've been violated all over again.

'Yeah, some of it was. And most of my friends. This kind of stuff, it's a bit like having braces for women of my generation.'

'It's very well written,' Nick says. Is he trying to patronise me? Maybe they want to remind me of how young I am.

'Thanks.'

'We really like it ...' says Matt. 'But we think if we develop it further, it should have more of a USP.'

'Unique selling point,' Nick says. Yep, thanks for that, Nick. Of course I know what USP stands for – I have finished my GCSEs.

'You know, we were wondering if there was a way of also getting the perspective of you being Alastair Campbell's daughter into the script. You know, could the lead – Bobbie? – be the daughter of a famous political figure?' Have they read the script?

'Her mum is a Labour politician,' I say.

'Yep, sure, but I think it being her dad speaks more to your truth.' Oh, okay, and when a man pitches a programme about the end of the world, do you ask him to make it 'not the end of the world', because that's closer to his truth?

I stay silent for a while.

'Hmm ... interesting ...' I say eventually. 'I feel that slightly takes away from the point of the script, which is showing the nuances in consent for women. I think making it about my dad makes it about my dad, and about men, do you know what I mean? This is a script about women.'

'Yeah, I'm just thinking, when we take this to commissioners, they'll want you to be doing a show about who your dad is, because, to be blunt, it's the most interesting thing about you.'

'Yeah, I'm well aware of how interesting it is. I know him really well, and he is interesting. I've developed scripts about that, but this feels like a film about women.' 'Well done, Gracie. Stick to your guns,' I can hear my mum saying.

'Mmmm, I'm not sure that's true, though,' Matt says. 'This is also a film about men, isn't it?' He puts on a sad face. Oh, I get it, he wants it to be about men because otherwise he can't back it.

'It's about men's lack of respect to women, sure.' It's obvious Matt doesn't like being disagreed with, and Horatio flashes into my mind. Matt is looking at me like he wants to push me in a pool. The two men sit in silence, looking at anything around us but me. I visualise being in the swimming pool that Matt has pushed me into. I'm floating around, naked. Two women walk past our table, which makes the silence even more unbearable.

'Soooo ... what else are you working on at the moment?' Nick asks.

'I'm actually making a feminist prank show at the moment for Channel 4.' They both laugh.

'What's a feminist prank?' Matt asks, still laughing. 'Do you just rape a guy for half an hour and call that an episode?'

They both laugh again. And this might shock you, but I laugh, too.

•

When I realised what Matt had said to me, I decided I needed to ruin his life. Okay, no. I just had to get out of that building before I started crying. I checked the time and told them I had to leave, politely thanking the two men for meeting me. We agreed we would 'be in touch'. Even though it was clear I'd rather touch all the micro-penises in the world than be in touch with Matt again.

I left their offices with a rash all over my body. Sometimes this happens when I'm having an allergic reaction to people I don't like. I considered I might be overreacting. Maybe he was just making a joke, and I hadn't understood it. Maybe I'm not actually that funny. No, the only funny thing about him was that his head looked like my vibrator. I called Anna to find out if it would make her as mad as it had made me.

'You are fucking KIDDING me,' Anna said.

'Nope.'

'Oh my god, Grace, you have to tell someone about this. Can you tell your agents?'

'I dunno. This guy is a big deal in comedy.'

'Yeah, but he probably says this shit all the time.'

'I know, but ... no, what the fuck am I saying "but" for? It was rank. He was so grim – he looked like that guy who followed us home from Dalston once.'

'Oh yes, the guy who told us his dad was Rupert Murdoch,' she said.

'Yeah, but he didn't know who Wendi Deng was, looool.'

'So, what are you gonna do?' Anna asked.

'I dunno, there's not much I can do.'

'You can refuse to work with him.'

'Yeah, but then what if people start talking about me like I'm a spoilt little Veruca Salt?'

'Grace, who gives a shit?'

Anna was right, but I did really give a shit. Not just about this, but about how this story fitted in with so many I'd started hearing from other women. There was a creeping sense in me that although this was a horrible thing that had happened, it wasn't as bad as some of the things that have happened to other people in film and TV and comedy. This industry was clearly suffering from a plague of inadequate men who aimed to make women feel uncomfortable and insignificant. And I was fucking furious. Even if I tried to confront the fact that this man had made a terrible comment, masked as a joke, which felt personal to my rape, what would happen to him? Matt would probably just carry on being Matt. He would go onto his WhatsApp group called Dickheads Anonymous for TV, and he'd tell all the other gatekeepers to stop working with women like me who 'can't take a joke'. Then I'd be banished from the industry before I'd even met Graham Norton. And the same is true of all the other women who've told me similar stories. Everyone knew nothing would be done, that the men had all the power. And what made that realisation even fucking worse was that it didn't look like anything was changing, even when we did kick up a fuss.

When I started making *Riot Girls*, the feminist prank show where, to Matt's horror, no one was raped, I wanted to make it my mission to do things differently. From the very beginning I decided I had to be on the defensive at all times. I was Gary Neville in the FA Cup final, always ready to defend the squad.

I don't wanna say too much about the process of making this show, because I worked with a lot of incredible people. I had the best time with Sophie, Cam and Jen, the three other comedians. But as long as there were men around, the bullshit marching band was trying to put on a show with the aim of killing my vibe.

I'd worked with a production company to pitch the show to Channel 4, and Sophie, Cam and Jen had been part of the writing crew when we were pitching. In the early stages of development, it had been agreed that if this got commissioned, the production company and channel were committed to this production having an all-female crew. This was a huge deal, because film crews are full of men employing their mates in departments throughout the set.

Also, because it was a feminist show, it was important that the crew wasn't just female, but a cross-over of all intersections of women, because then it would be representing women properly, and not just be some tokenistic shit.

But slowly, every few days, the producer would call me, sounding as if there had been another death in the family. 'Unfortunately, we couldn't find a female director', 'Sadly there were no available female line producers' or 'Annoyingly, none of the female cinematographers available have the right experience.'

All of these roles were being given to ... straight men instead. Straight men who were good at their job and had all the right experience, but they weren't what was promised. It's like if I go to a restaurant and order penne arrabbiata, but then they come out with lamb chops – I'm gonna complain, aren't I? I was wholly unsatisfied with what was happening.

I didn't buy the idea that there were NO available women in London – a city with a population of eleven million people – who could work on this show at that time. In fact, I know it was bullshit, because since that experience I've met so many women who do those roles and have so often struggled to get jobs. So the question is, were they not looking or were they deliberately not finding?

And then I was like fuck, shit the bucket. Or the bed. What is that phrase? Well, it came to me: this is what this industry is. Mediocre men getting picked over exceptional women, all because it's easier to just hire people you know. And if you didn't think women had talent at film school, so you only worked with men and made friends with those men, then chances are when you're in a position of power, you're only going to have men in your network. Hello, Alfie, meet your future self, Matt.

How often have you heard someone in a position of power say, 'We'll do better. We'll hire more women in senior positions. We'll hire more Black people in senior positions. We'll become more diverse.'

And you believe them, just like you believe your toxic boyfriend who's telling you he'll change, he'll do better. But he will always disappoint you because he doesn't want to change. He wants you to get off his back, so he'll say anything, and then he'll go to the pub with his friends and he'll forget the promise he's just made you. But then you'll come in, order a gin, sit down in front of them and say, 'HELLO, may I please have a refund on those pathetic excuses? Because your lies are as mouldy as the jam that's been in my grandma's cupboard since 1958.'

It's so easy for men at the top to make false promises and then go back to their little gang of people they want to let in – people who support their efforts to maintain the status quo in order to reduce any risk of their mediocrity being revealed. Except they don't realise their mediocrity, because they are surrounded by people who say, 'Good idea, mate, absolute corker,' and that feels warm and fuzzy and certainly much nicer than having women looking at them with palpable disdain. Why would they want to let anyone else in? It's so lovely and average how it is.

I have benefited from these power structures, too. There are so many white women getting opportunities over Black and Brown women who are more deserving, and that's because of this one system of power, which white people have historically not wanted to change because it helps them.

I'm sure some of you reading this will have experienced similar things. All industries have pricks like Matt at the top, making anyone who doesn't look like them feel uncomfortable and unwelcome. Whether you're in a Zoom conference call and can't seem to get a word in, or you're in a company watching three sub-standard men get promoted before you, or you suddenly feel like your boss values you and is engaged in your work and then they invite you for dinner, and you realise they don't care about what you think. Then you feel ashamed because you're not valued, so you assume you're not working hard enough. But the people around you being promoted leave before you. And you want it to make sense, but it doesn't.

I already ranked men pretty low. Like a pound's worth of Bitcoin. And I didn't always have to work with men

– I'm lucky to be able to choose. But now, I decided that I would put working with men – from Alfie, to Matt, to everyone in between – in the 'bad for my mental health' list, along with drum and bass, cocaine and stalking my boyfriend's exes on Instagram.

In fact, by the time I was twenty-four, I'd written off all men . . . apart from one.

MAKING A PODCAST WITH MY DAD

I wonder if my dad ever looked at me when I was a baby and considered that one day, when I was older and could walk and talk and get dressed on my own, we would work together. Did he ever look at baby me, the spitting image of Susan Boyle (the Scottish *Britain's Got Talent* singer) with my ginger curls and a permanent red face, and think, 'One day, me and this girl might have a podcast together'? Not just any podcast, but one about Football and Feminism? Obviously, no one knew what a podcast was in the Nineties, so that would have been a mind fuck to begin with.

> Hey, people of the Nineties, one day you will have this thing called a podcast. A podcast is basically like a radio show but more specific, and there will be a phrase that goes, 'Oh, there's a podcast for everything,' which there is! Including the most popular type of podcast, the

crime-solving serial-killer genre. Also, everyone you
know will make one. That guy you once met in Venice,
yep, he's got one! Your hairdresser, yep, he's got one.
Even your mum has one.

I don't think Nineties Alastair Campbell would have
liked the idea of a podcast, and he definitely wouldn't have
believed that one day he'd be on any sort of platform talking about feminism.

Back when I was born, in the mid-Nineties, my dad
was one of the most powerful people in the country, and
he rated himself as really progressive – and in loads of
ways he was. New Labour progressed LGBTQ+ rights
massively by introducing civil partnerships, scrapping
Section 28 (which was preventing teachers from talking
about homosexuality in schools), and much more. New
Labour introduced the minimum wage, and created all-
women shortlists to boost female representation in
Parliament. But still, my dad was to feminism what I am to
football: amateur.

He thought that because he worked with women, and
hired women, there was nothing more he had to do to help
women. Luckily, my dad had me to call him out. Yes, the
sun shines out of my arse, and feminism pours out of my
mouth like Cîroc vodka. Much higher brow than Glen's.

When I was fourteen, I started fighting with my parents,
who, I had realised, were patriarchy-enabling feminists.

They were letting the patriarchy thrive like a yeast infection all through our home. My dad didn't do anything around the house. He didn't cook, rarely cleaned, he'd even make a fuss if my mum asked him to take the bins out!

And then around that time, I clocked that my mum was letting my brothers get away with the same thing. They wouldn't cook. They wouldn't clean. They didn't take the bins out. But . . . wait, I was . . . at least, I was doing some of it. Mum, before you call every single person who's bought this book to contradict that, give me a break. I *was* cooking. I *was* washing up. But I never took the bins out because I have a severe phobia of bin juice. Fun fact: I've never taken the bins out in my life, even now, in the flat I live in, I never take the bins out. I just always get Bae, or any of my friends to do it. You may all steal this life-hack, unless you are one of my friends, in which case, it's bin day tomorrow, where are you?

But I did things. And not because my mum asked me to all the time; I offered to help her. At first, I liked this. It felt like mum and I had our own thing. While the boys and my dad retreated into the living room to watch the football, we would do women's things, you know?

Once the novelty wore thin, I took off my fog glasses, looked around the kitchen and saw a painting of the 1960s! Why am I here loading the dishwasher and scrubbing the baking tray, when they are in there talking about

Manchester United's performance? Should I just pretend I like football? No, I don't like football, and it shouldn't be my mum's job alone to do this stuff.

'Mum, why don't Rory and Calum do anything in the kitchen?'

'Because they won't.'

'Why don't you make them? When I have kids I'm gonna make them do everything.'

'I don't know. Ask them.'

'I think it's because you're enabling the patriarchy. You and Dad say you're feminists.' My mum looked exasperated by this conversation. No wonder – she was busy doing all the housework and working full-time. I was making the fatal error of misplacing my rage.

I turned on my dad. My nurturing, encouraging, supportive dad. Little did he know, he'd created a monster. When I was a child, he adored my opinionated, confident, loud temperament – I was often using it to defend him – but now the student was taking on the master, and he went on the defensive. He'd joke and tell me to 'stop nagging', or some other inane trope, which made me feel a sense of rage that I cherish to this day. It was obvious that despite my mum being a feminist, she was too tolerant when my dad said he 'couldn't' do things.

My dad and I battled back and forth, neither surrendering much ground, mostly because we had greater enemies to face together. Then one day, when I was twenty-two, I got a text from him: 'Hosting a show on LBC about feminism this aft.'

'LOL. You're not a feminist!'

'It's a show about whether or not men can be feminists. Listen in.'

I did more than that. He was taking calls from the public.

AC: 'Let's go to Grace in Camden.'

GC: 'Hi, Dad . . .'

'Hello, Grace.' He laughs. 'You're a feminist. Can a man be a feminist?'

'Yes . . . I think a man can be a feminist. But I think that if they truly want to be one, they really need to unpick things that they've adopted naturally because of the way that society teaches them to behave. So I think that for a man to be a feminist it's a lot more than just saying you're a feminist . . . I've thought of some examples with you, which I'm gonna talk about.'

Dad laughs.

'Firstly, you still call women "birds" . . . You do it when you're around men, I've observed. Women aren't birds. Birds are birds. Birds can fly. Women can't fly.'

'And I like birds,' my dad says. I feel like I won this point.

'And also, this thing about doing stuff in the household is really interesting, because I've noticed that what you do, which a lot of men do, is you make up the excuse of "I can't", so you'll say, "I don't know how to do the laundry," or "I don't know how to use the coffee machine, so I can't."'

You may recognise this tactic from my bad tea/bad head tactic, but I hope you'll agree that I had slightly more justification for using it.

'And instead of saying you can't,' I went on, 'just learn how to use an espresso machine, because they've made them so easy that you could use them. And thirdly, you still get grossed out when I talk about my period.'

My dad found my rant hilarious. He loves a public dispute, as you might know. He loves to trend on Twitter. He replied to me, live on radio, by saying, 'Yeah, yeah, stop nagging me, Grace. How many Burnley players can you name?'

The clip of me telling off my dad got loads of attention, because, as my mum says, me and my dad never do anything by halves. After this, I got hundreds of messages from girls my age saying that they'd had that exact same argument with their dads at Christmas, on Sundays, on holidays. Most girls who have their fathers in their lives will have had those same skin-itchingly frustrating beefs with their dads about gender. These are important conversations that we should be having with our dads. If we're lucky enough to have them in our lives, they take the responsibility of raising us. But now, if we love them, we have a responsibility to update their iOS and raise them to be versions of themselves that are adapted to the times.

So after this, we decided to make a podcast together. At that point, Dad was having an existential crisis about what his purpose in the world was. He didn't have a role in the Labour Party any more, and he felt that, compared to how much power he'd once had, he was a nobody now. So he wanted a new 'thing', and I thought it would be fun and would help boost my profile. Nepotism.

But if he wasn't my dad, and I wasn't his daughter, I think we would have sacked each other on our first day. We would have decided that this working relationship was never going to work, and we would have agreed to 'be in touch', when we had no intention of reaching out. He didn't like how argumentative, stubborn and arrogant I was, and I kept reminding him that I'd learnt this bullishness from him.

When we started recording the podcast, my dad became obsessed with how loud my voice was. I've always spoken loudly. This is a book, so you can't hear how loudly I'm speaking, unless you're listening to the audiobook, in which case I assume you've turned the volume down. My average volume is like the Pyramid Stage at Glastonbury.

For my whole life, my dad's been interrupting me and sticking his fingers in his ears, then asking me, 'Why the fuck do you have to speak like you're on stage, Grace?' My answer was that I am the stage, I am the microphone and I am the voice.

But when we were recording the first episode with Ed Miliband, my dad interrupted the recording ten minutes in to say, 'Grace, can you stop laughing so loudly. It's irritating for all of us.' This made me laugh even more, and if you haven't heard me laugh, it's like an excited koala bear.

'Is it irritating you, Ed?' I asked Ed.

'Not at all,' Ed said. It's such a shame he didn't win because of a bacon sandwich. I really like him.

My dad and I fight as much as the Kardashians fight with their mum, Kris Jenner. We've had so many ridiculous arguments over the course of the three seasons. I don't want to explain them because I know my dad will read this and have a different version of what happened, and then he'll call me up and that will escalate into another argument, and we won't speak for a day, and I just want to be as relaxed as possible, so best not to.

The difference between my dad and Matt the Twat is that, firstly, my dad isn't an arsehole, and secondly, my dad wants to learn how to be a better feminist. My dad will, if he's spoken to calmly (which isn't a natural trait of mine), listen to me. I feel in control when I'm working with him, because I trust him. You should be able to work with people you trust, too. If you don't trust who you work with, and they don't make you feel safe, seek out people you *do* trust, find female mentors, build a network of people you know want the best for you. Never be ashamed of taking what you want from work and building the team you want, when that is possible. Some people might make you feel you're not as good as them. Those people are usually men, and I'm sure you can guess what I'm about to say: a lot of men are twats.

•

About a year after I met Matt the Twat, I was at my yoga studio in Camden. I was at my favourite Friday-lunchtime vinyasa flow class, namaste-ing and getting zen before a big weekend of boozing. I'm lying on the mat, doing my warm-up stretches, showing off my handstands, that kind of thing, and I sense someone put their mat down behind me. I glance through the crack between my legs and see that it's him. It's Matt the Twat. No one could mistake that head.

He looks at me – that same look he gave me before, like he's about to push me in a pool. I look back, with the face that I pull when I get chatted up in the street. He's ruined my zen, so I'm gonna ruin his. The class starts with a chant. I chant louder than anyone in the room. I am louder than him now. I am bigger than him. And when we start moving, I did what I've dreamt of doing ever since I met him. I got into my downward dog position and I fanny farted into his puny little face. I knew being able to fanny fart on demand would come in handy one day.

A REIMAGINATION OF MY MEETING

I'm waiting on a sticky leather sofa in the reception of a production company's office. There's a mural behind the receptionist's desk, which I can't stop staring at. It's Dolly Parton. Her face is magically Dollyish, and next to her there's one of her most famous quotes: 'Find out who you are and do it on purpose.'

That quote would be so cheesy if Dolly hadn't said it. Can you imagine if I posted that quote on my Instagram? My friends would rip the shit out of me forever. But it's Dolly, and I'm sitting here reading it in her voice, and imagining her smile, and thinking *j'adore* with all of my heart, and that if I ever got the chance to meet her, I would love to get drunk with her.

I've been told by my agents that I'm meeting two women, both of whom liked my script and wanted to meet me.

From the vibe of the office, I feel like I'd be popular here. I'd fit in with the pastel wall colours and the motivational quotes. Maybe I'd go as far as teaching a weekly yoga class. The two women float into the reception. They both look excited to see me, so I match that and show them my highest level of excitement. They look like a couple of babes, the kind of women I'd meet in the queue of a pub toilet, and we'd start bitching together and end up getting drunk and dancing all night to Sister Sledge.

A reimagination of my meeting

'Hi, Grace! I'm Martha,' says the brunette one, who's wearing a leather jacket indoors, which makes me think she's tough.

'I'm Nicola,' says the other one, who's got a blonde bob and tattoos all the way up her arms, the biggest one being of Marilyn Monroe, and walking alongside Marilyn is a herd of baby elephants.

The two women lead me into a meeting room. They ask me if I want a drink and I ask for a green tea as well as a coffee. It's 10 a.m. and I usually double up around this time of day.

MARTHA
Grace, it's so nice to finally meet you.

GRACE
So nice. I have really bad thrush, by the way, so if you notice me rubbing around, that's what I'm doing.
They laugh.

NICOLA
Oh, don't worry, babes, we've all been there, rubbing our fanny around on the chair in a driving lesson. Or was that just me?

GRACE
I got thrush in a driving test! And I'm convinced he failed me because he thought I was scrubbing my minge on the seat.

MARTHA

You've got amazing hair. My daughter has similar hair to that, but she rolls in mud so often there's no point trying to make it look good.

GRACE

Well, send her to me when she's older and I can tell her all the tricks.

MARTHA

So, how are you finding life? You're quite young, aren't you?

GRACE

I'm twenty-one.

NICOLA

Oh wow, when I was twenty-one I was still working at TGI Friday's and stealing curly fries at the end of my shift and trading them for a bottle of rosé at the shop.

GRACE

I love that for you.

MARTHA

So, let's talk about *Sweetie*. We absolutely loved it.

GRACE

Oh ma God, thanks!

MARTHA

I'm presuming it was autobiographical?

A reimagination of my meeting

GRACE

Yep, it was, but also, you know, that kind of stuff happens to all women my age.

NICOLA

Oh we know, babe, and you're amazing for writing about it.

MARTHA

For sure, reading this made me feel so protective of my daughter when she's older. She's five now and it made me just want to somehow stunt her growth.

GRACE

Can you do that?

MARTHA

No, no, figuratively. Because your writing just made me want to protect her – and the lead character, I felt so protective of her.

NICOLA

How did it feel to write this?

GRACE

Before I wrote it, I felt like I was really constipated, and then afterwards I just felt lighter. It was the best dump.
They laugh.

NICOLA

And what else are you working on at the moment?

GRACE

I'm making a feminist prank show for Channel 4.

MARTHA

Ha! It's about time men got punk'd.

GRACE

Men are punking themselves as we speak.

And then we had a huge hug, went to Glastonbury together and took shrooms. Unfortunately, we fell out when we were high and I thought Martha had stolen my hand sanitiser.

WOMEN WHO DON'T SUPPORT OTHER WOMEN CAN'T CUM

Before I talk about the women who have made me, I have to talk about **Ashley**.

And before I talk about Ashley, I have to introduce one of my most important friends. Stella – my wild, gorgeous and mentally unstable friend – was a lot like me. The only difference between Stella and me was that Stella was a horse. Stella lived with other horses on a farm in Essex. Between the ages of twelve and sixteen, I went to see Stella multiple times a week. My mum would drive me there on weekends, and I'd spend days pretending I wasn't a North Londoner. I was at a farm talking to animals about the big questions in life. Like how do flying ants always know it's flying ant day? And why don't we fall over more in the shower? I'm grateful to Stella because she showed me that there was more to adolescence than drinking Glen's Vodka and smoking Mayfair cigarettes.

At the stables, I made some horse friends. These are human friends that I only socialised with when horses were around. Ashley, whose horse Barley was in the stable next door to my baby Stella, was one of my horse friends. Ashley was a proper horse girl. She wore horse clothes even when she wasn't horsing, as a mark to other people that she rides horses. Ashley's favourite colour was dark purple, which I always thought had very 'retirement home' vibes, but she insisted that purple was 'the new pink' and I had to respect her dedication to the cause.

Ashley's family lived in a really nice house next to the stables. Her dad had a construction company, which meant he was also really good at doing odd jobs at the stables, unlike my dad, who covered his eyes whenever I picked up Stella's poo. Ashley's mum, Karen, was a proper show mum. If this were America, Karen would have somehow got Ashley onto *The Ellen Show* by now. Karen used to film all of Ashley's horse-riding performances, and afterwards she'd make Ashley sit down with her on the sofa like she was José Mourinho and watch back the performance, giving 'constructive feedback'. Ashley had no choice but to listen to her mum mug her off for an hour, which can't have been fun.

Ashley had a bit of an attitude problem, which I couldn't really blame her for, her mum was very controlling. But Ashley also had a mean streak. The first time she met Tyler, she told me she thought she was rude, which was a first for Tyler, who is virtually impossible to dislike. Then Ashley also told me she thought my mum was 'a stuck-up snob'. This offended me deeply, but I didn't want to have a fight with Ashley, so I just replied by saying, 'Yeah, she loves Prada.' I felt guilty about saying that about my mum for days.

Ashley was also very competitive with me. I didn't want to become a professional horse rider, because to be honest adult horse people are fucking weird, but I think because Ashley wanted to be a professional horse rider so much, and her mum was putting so much pressure on her, her natural instinct was to compete with me. I get it.

Ashley loved to chat shit about me and Stella. She used to tell me that Stella was too 'deranged' to ever win shows, and when I told her I couldn't give a shit about winning shows, because I was gonna be a famous actress, Ashley accused me of lying. But I stayed friends with Ashley because she was a reliable friend at the farm, she could be funny and her parents had a horse lorry, which was useful for transporting the horses when we competed.

Our horses were really different. Ashley's horse, Barley, was a plank of wood. Barley was simple, he was calm and he was adorable, but he wasn't as complex as Stella and therefore him and Ashley didn't quite bond like Stella and I. Stella, my baby, had lots of trauma. The horse dealer had told us that she'd experienced a lot of emotional damage, and we had to pay for her in cash because that's all the seller would accept. This made me very protective of her. Stella was spooked by a lot of things. She hated men – she was always on edge when a man was around, even if it was my dad; she turned spikey. Honestly, what an icon! She was also terrified of anyone other than me touching her behind her ears. This was the warmest and softest part of her body, but it was covered in aggressive scars, I assumed from being abused.

She was also absolutely terrified of plastic bags. Lots of horses are. When you've lived in grass fields your whole life, you'll see a Sainsbury's bag for life and think, 'What the fuck is this spaceship flying over me?' When Stella saw plastic bags she turned into a bucking bronco.

Stella and I were really connected. If Netflix had existed then, maybe they would have made a documentary: *Grace and Stella, Best Friends Forever*. Stella just got me, you know?

Anyway, one day we were on our way to a showjumping competition. Ashley's dad, Steve, was driving. Steve was quiet most of the time – he always looked like he wanted to be somewhere else, but Karen had him under her thumb. Karen was filing her nails while chewing gum ferociously. 'Ash, if you don't win today, you're never gonna get into the Lee Valley Championship, and you want that so much, don't you?'

'Yeah, of course I do, Mum.'

'Right, well, it would be a lot of money wasted if you didn't,' Karen said, laughing. Which was true – horses are a very expensive luxury, and I think Karen wanted Barley to be as value for money as possible. She was a competitive mum, but she was also obviously worried about the money they'd spent. I could see she was making Ashley nervous.

We got to the competition, parked the lorry and I started doing Stella's hair and make-up. All of our accessories were baby blue. That was our colour, because we both looked great in it. I plaited her mane with baby-blue hairbands. Then I put some shiny coat spray on her, put her baby-blue saddle cloth on, gave her some carrots and we were ready.

Ashley went first. I was standing with Stella where the van was parked, watching her from afar. Ashley started off well, but then she knocked down two poles in a row. As soon as she'd finished and left the paddock, Karen took Barley off her and whispered something in her ear. Ashley looked crushed, and I wanted to go over and tell her that it's 'just a horse show'. But I'm up now.

I go out and I'm nervous. Stella is a babe, but she's a sensitive soul who is easily triggered, and I don't want some bloke to come along and freak her out.

We start off well, acing the first three jumps. Stella can sense that I'm happy. And she's happy because I'm happy. Stella respects me more than any lover ever will. But then, when we turn back to come down the other side of the paddock, I see Ashley reaching into her mum's handbag and pulling out a blue plastic bag. She starts looking through the plastic bag and my stomach sinks, then Stella picks up on my energy and her ears prick up, and she hears the plastic bag.

And Ashley is still rustling the bag. Why is it taking her so fucking long to take something out of a plastic bag? Has she suddenly got impaired vision? Is the bag full of fucking wads of cash??

Now we're closer to her and Stella has noticed the bag in Ashley's hand, and she's panicking. Ashley rustles it again, and now Stella's pissed. I'm watching Ashley and I see her glance up at Stella, assessing the damage, before rustling the bag more. Stella starts bucking and rearing and freaking the fuck out, because she's been triggered. I manage to stay on because I've got good at handling her moments.

We got disqualified from the competition. I wasn't mad at Stella at all – my poor baby, it's not her fault. But I was mad at Ashley. Ashley wanted me to lose. I've never been able to look at a plastic bag since. I mean, not literally, but I do get pangs. Also, they're terrible for the environment, so maybe Stella was onto something.

After Ashley tried to trigger Stella's PTSD to beat me in an amateur horse show, in which she came fifth, I carried on being friends with her. I carried on being friends with Ashley for two reasons. Firstly, I didn't want to fall out with the person who had access to my horse's stable. She could fill Stella's stable with plastic bags when I wasn't there. But also, I knew I was guilty of similar, competitive behaviour in my life. I understood that growing up around alpha men had made me like that, so I had to understand that Ashley's behaviour was a symptom of her homelife, too.

I didn't tell the girls at school about my antics with Ashley. I didn't think it was too big a deal. At the time, we were being taught that 'this is just what girls are like'. Oh, girls, they're so fake, they're such bitches to each other, they all hate each other.

That was what the patriarchy wanted us to think. I have a theory that the patriarchy was running a secret, well-executed campaign called 'Make Girls Bitches Again', which oppressed young women by teaching them that the only way to act with their female peers was to compete with them. The patriarchy knew that if they did this, it would slow us down. Because when women aren't support-ing other women, the patriarchy thrives like a Lush bath bomb.

Boys upheld this idea that women were bitches, by call-ing us bitches at every opportunity. And in everything we watched, being a bitch was glorified. From Regina George, to Blair Waldorf, to Lauren Conrad, being a bitch was synonymous with being hot and popular. It was a must-have accessory. We thought that women had to be full-time, double-dosed, whipped-cream-on-top bitches, *xoxo Gossip Girl*. And as you know, I was no exception to the rule. I was insecure and so I acted all tough because I wanted people to respect me.

There were more friends like Ashley, sure. I have had plenty of passive-aggressive friendships with other women that haven't made me feel good. I've had relationships with women where I've been a total bitch. Some friendships have brought out the terrible side of me. And a bit like me and orange, I don't suit it – it makes me look awful. Same with toxic friendships – they make me a bitchy person. They've made me be the type of woman I dislike.

And it was through these friendships that I realised my life was nicer when I wasn't trying to emulate Blair Waldorf. Supporting and being supported by the women in my life has completely transformed me. It's made my immune system stronger, it's improved my mental health, my skin has got better and, of course, my orgasms have improved.

I look at male friendships and I feel so desperately sorry for them. They go to football matches and the pub and occasionally pat each other on the back and say, 'It's okay, mate.' No wonder they have to take out their sadness on women. No wonder most men make their girlfriends their part-time therapists. No wonder men resolve to fighting instead of communicating with each other. They're taught to be emotionally unavailable.

The more I saw female friendships as these beacons of positivity and strength, the more I saw why so many men were colossal arseholes. While a lot of men have rejected me in my life, so many women have accepted me, and that's the drug I'd rather be addicted to. If I was writing a book about all the women I've loved, it would take up many, many volumes. Please look forward to my next book deal. But for now, let me mention a few close to my heart.

I met **Scarlett** when I was twenty-one years old. We knew of each other, in the way that Facebook makes sure you always know of the people you share mutual friends with. Scarlett Curtis. Everyone that was a mutual friend of hers raved about her. I was a little jealous of how cool she sounded. I decided I needed to be her friend.

We finally met at a photoshoot for *Elle* magazine, which was profiling new young writers. I was nervous that day. It was my first photoshoot, and I was obsessively thinking about how fat my stomach was and how much my face made me look like Phil Mitchell's (of *EastEnders*) cousin. I was unphotogenic then because I hadn't spent enough time looking in the mirror and nailing my good angles. Yes, you may stop reading for a minute to go and look at yours, if you care – maybe you don't. So I was convinced that they'd take pictures of me, and that when they looked at them on the computer they'd all start to laugh at how much like a thumb I looked, and then they'd refuse to print me in the magazine.

Scarlett came in when I was getting my make-up done. She was being profiled as a writer, too. Everything she was wearing was pink, and it looked expensive. Her face had a natural glow to it, which made her radiate this unfiltered look of positivity. And she looked excited to see me.

'Hi, Grace, I'm Scarlett!!! You look so cool!'

'Oh thanks, so do you. I'm so nervous,' I whisper.

'You don't look nervous at all! I've been so nervous about this all week.'

'Well, you're amazing, and it's so nice to finally meet you.'

'Honestly, the only reason I did this was because I wanted to meet you,' she said.

And just like that, I wasn't Phil Mitchell's cousin on the photoshoot, I was Scarlett's friend.

The next week we met up for lunch at my favourite restaurant in Belsize Park, Chez Bob. Friend dates, in my opinion, are much more exciting than romantic ones. There are no nerves, wondering, 'Oh, are we going to have to kiss?' Friend dates can go one of two ways: they are either awful and you never have to see them again apart from occasionally on the street in Soho and you can just pretend you're on the phone; or, over the course of lunch, you forge a bond with another woman so deep you feel like you're gaining unconditional love right away. That's what happened with Scarlett.

We had a lot in common. Scarlett grew up in the public eye, too. Her parents are film-makers Richard Curtis and Emma Freud. We both had Famous Dad Syndrome; our obsessions and levels of respect for our fathers meant that we could never find men who we felt our dads would approve of. I know that our life experiences are very unique, but I'm sure a lot of you reading can relate to having daddy issues.

Over some post-lunch Diet Cokes, Scarlett just got straight to the point: 'Well, I would really like to be friends with you.' Take a second and imagine a man saying anything like this. Saying they want to be your friend, your boyfriend, your part-time lover. This was so much more exciting than an actual date, because we were committing on our second meeting. 'I was so intimidated by you when I met you,' she said. 'But now I see that's just because you're really cool.'

'It's so weird, because I feel like we've known each other for years,' I said, in a show of immediate intimacy I'd unlearnt over ten years of interactions with men.

'No, I feel like we've lived this whole life together.' And suddenly 'this whole life' felt like a very good thing.

There are only two things I'm into collecting in the world. One: sunglasses. I hope one day my sunglasses collection will be displayed in an exhibition at the V&A. And the second thing I pride myself on is my group of friends, and I hope that they will also be in said exhibition at the V&A.

Being wrapped up in this bundle of obsessive female friendship with Scarlett also made me realise how lucky I've been for most of my life to be so consistently held by my best friends. This was never more obvious than when I took the plunge and decided to do stand-up comedy . . .

•

Anna, Tyler and I are marching down Chamberlayne Road in Kensal Rise. Kensal Rise is like North-west London gentrification personified. Lots of yummy mummies in yoga trousers casually strolling past us with their babies in Bugaboos. Lots of bars opening for the evening. It's one of those gorgeous spring evenings in April when the dark winter finally feels over, and everyone in London is drunk in a beer garden. My underboobs are dripping in sweat.

'Ah, fuck me, I'm sure I've got piles. Piles of piles. Piles of piles of piles,' I say.

'It's just nerves,' Tyler says.

'Mmm, no. I think I have food poisoning, Ty. We ate fish last night,' I say.

'Grace, you're not getting out of this,' says Tyler.

'Yeah, and honestly, food poisoning? Basic excuse,' Anna adds.

All day, in between sobbing and shitting my memory out on the toilet in my parents' house, I've been having a panic attack about tonight. Tonight is a monumental moment for me. Tonight I'm ABBA at the final of Eurovision.

Tonight, I'm doing stand-up for the first time. I'm doing a five-minute comedy set at an open-mic night at the Paradise, a club in Kensal Rise. Five minutes?! That's, like, half of ten minutes. And ten minutes is a sixth of an hour. So, basically, I'm performing for a fucking hour!!! I'm going to throw up.

I have tried out my jokes on Tyler and Anna hundreds of times now, but I'm still convinced I'll get up there and forget I'm supposed to be funny and perform a eulogy for my own funeral. The funeral of my stand-up career. She started, April 2018, and she finished five minutes later, April 2018.

'You're gonna be amazing,' says Tyler.

'Do you wanna go through the set again?' Anna said.

'Yep.' I stop dramatically. My mouth is so dry I feel like I could swallow my tongue if I don't concentrate on holding it in the middle of my mouth. I drop my belongings on the floor.

'Open with fanny fart. Then Tiree, my Scottish grandma. Monogamy. One-night stands. Being single. Getting the morning-after pill. Theresa May's cum face.'

'Great, great, great, you've got it.'

The girls reassure me that the set is going to be epic, but when we get to the Paradise, I can barely see anyone inside. I thought there'd be a queue outside, a red carpet perhaps. I'd dreamt of my debut gig for so long. I expected a crowd.

'Why am I doing this? No one's even here!!' I ask the girls.

'Because you've got to start somewhere!' Tyler says.

I'm too terrified to go in, so we waste more time. Tyler smokes a cigarette – Sterling Dual (this was back when menthol cigarettes were a thing) – and I put more concealer on the spots around my mouth.

Then we go in. I was convinced we'd get in there and loads of my ex-lovers would be sitting front row because they'd somehow found out that I was doing stand-up – Dickheads Anonymous on a school trip, ready to heckle me. So I'm shocked but not disappointed to find that my debut gig has an audience of two people: Anna and Tyler. There are eight other men in the room, but they are all performing. When we walk in, making a lot of noise, none of them addresses me. Dickheads everywhere.

The host is an older man with thick glasses called Jonny. He has his greasy hair in a long, thin, ratty ponytail. 'Hi, I'm Grace,' I say.

'Hi, Rosie, I'm Jonny. You're late so you'll be on last.' I don't correct that he got my name wrong. I was too focused on the fact that I was going last.

This would be great if there was a crowd of people who were getting more and more drunk over the course of the night; they'd be loose by the time I went on. But we are the crowd, and there isn't much chance of me being any looser by the time I go on. The other acts have to stay, that's the rule, but I'm not sure these eight men will like my jokes about fanny farts and men being trash.

Anna and Tyler get a bottle of rosé and a packet of crisps, and I drink water non-stop. Tiny little sips so there is no risk of me wetting myself on stage.

One by one, the men go onto the stage and tell jokes about their wives, or their dicks being small, or the fact that they're still living with their parents. Us three laugh nervously at all of it because we think it's polite, but also because if we don't they'll be performing to the sound of Anna rustling her crisp packet.

'And now,' Jonny says, 'for Rosieeeee Campbell.'

I clap, forgetting that to him, I am now called Rosie. It's me. Fuck.

'It's just us!' Anna says as I get up nervously. 'Perform to us.'

I get to the stage. I've never held a microphone before. It's so big and thick, and then I realise that the only thing I know to do with an object this shape is to seduce it. What would Dua Lipa do? Be Dua Lipa.

The lights are so bright I can't see any of the audience members. Anna and Tyler are cheering for me loudly like I'm a jock in an American high-school movie. 'GC! GC!!!!' they chant. I fire through the set. Every single joke, Anna and Tyler laugh. Really, their performance is incredible. They make it sound like this is the first time they've heard any of my jokes. I can't even hear that none of the men are laughing. I finish the set, and the girls give me a standing ovation, while the men watch us, confused, like we're drinking mugs of piss.

'You were just so good, babe,' says Tyler at the pub afterwards. 'Those basic creeps had nothing on you.'

'Their faces, I wish you could've seen, they were gutted when you started because it was game over. Bada bing, bada boom.'

•

After that night, between Anna, Tyler, Jack, Scarlett, Emily and Tara, I didn't go to a single gig alone for the first six months of my stand-up career. My venture into comedy was a team effort. We made an event of it, a bit like going to the Brandon Centre. This was our new mission, collectively. We went to so many gigs in parts of London we'd never been to before. Gigs in the backs of pubs. Gigs in sheds in gardens. I once did a gig in a cupboard. After each set, the girls would critique me in a way they knew I could handle. They knew that, when it comes to criticism, I'm like a mediocre man, so they'd approach it diplomatically, and each time I'd get better and better.

I always think about Ella Fitzgerald and Marilyn Monroe when I look back on that time. They were great friends, you know? Fitzgerald, the singer, met Monroe, the actress, in 1954, because Monroe was obsessed with Fitzgerald's voice and music, obviously.

Monroe, who was at this point at the peak of her superstardom, wanted to use her Hollywood status to help Fitzgerald's career. Fitzgerald was doing well, but in an America that still had segregation laws, she wasn't getting the gigs she wanted. Bigger, more glamorous, better paying clubs were refusing to bill Fitzgerald, claiming she wasn't sexy enough to perform there, but this was almost certainly because she was Black. When Monroe found out that Fitzgerald wasn't getting gigs at the Mocambo, a famous nightclub in LA, Monroe phoned up the owner and insisted they book her friend, and if they did, Monroe would sit in the front row every day. The club said yes. Fitzgerald's shows sold out so quickly – because it was Ella Fitzgerald – that the club added an extra two weeks to her run. Monroe kept her promise and sat in the front row every night.

This is friendship and female allyship. Monroe knew she could use her power to help a friend who wasn't granted the same privileges. You're probably wondering why I'm telling you this story, after talking about my two friends coming with me to all of my first stand-up gigs. How dare she!

I'm not comparing these two stories. Fitzgerald was working as a Black woman in a time when America's racism was legally binding. But I just love hearing about what happens when women support other women. You get Ella Fitzgerald in the mainstream. And you get Grace Campbell performing to ten people in an open-mic night.

Would I have continued doing stand-up in cupboards if the girls hadn't been coming with me every time? Definitely not. Would I have thought I was funny enough to do stand-up in the first place if my friends hadn't been telling me I absolutely was? No way. Does anything else matter in the world when you have friends who champion you like a horse they've bet their life fortune on? No, it certainly does not.

•

I'm in King's Cross station. I've got three suitcases; Bae is dutifully pulling two of them along while I look for my platform. He's not coming on the train with me. I am meeting my work wife, Scarlett. We can see Scarlett outside Leon. She's wearing a perfect outfit. Pink tracksuit with a gorgeous leather side bag and glitter extensions in her hair. She is a gorgeous, pink-haired pixie who always nails the comfy-chic attire.

Scarlett and I are taking the train to Edinburgh, where I will be living for a month as, you know, I'm doing the Edinburgh Fringe. Bae walks us to our platform, obviously devastated that I'm leaving. How could he not be? We snog goodbye.

Scarlett and I get on the train. As a surprise, Scarlett's upgraded us to first class because she knows that the only thing that calms my nerves is glamour. Scarlett, loyally, is coming with me for the whole month. She's dedicating her summer to making sure I don't have a nervous breakdown – and she knows that this is a possibility, because we are the gatekeepers of each other's mental health.

On the train she starts making plans for the next few days. 'So I've booked us in at yoga tomorrow. And I've sorted our yoga passes for the month. And I was thinking tonight we have dinner at the house?' Without Scarlett, I would have been on my way to Edinburgh, sobbing in economy about how much I was about to miss everyone in my life.

But Scarlett has supporting other women in her DNA. It's what genuinely makes her happy, and she's worked it into every element of her life and work. Being obsessed with women is what she loves to do, and I have been a lucky benefactor of this love. Without the ongoing support of my friends, my comedy career would never have started.

Scarlett was the first friend I had worked with, too, and it was refreshing not to be competing with her. That's what I was used to – with women who were doing similar things to me, I'd naturally feel I had to compete with them. Even if they had done nothing to suggest they were competing with me, it was just an instinct I had. It was the unnecessarily competitive side of me that came from the idolisation I had of men ... and from seeing men act like the only way is to win, and thinking that's what I had to be like. But Scarlett showed me that when you support the women around you, everything you're doing becomes a collective, team effort.

This was a game changer for me, realising that when you support other women, you can get so much more done, and the graft of work will never be a lonely one. And then my anxiety levels decreased and my orgasms became even more liberated. And you know what? Even more importantly, I could stop thinking about myself. It came as a shock to me, too, but this thing happened where, because I felt secure, and the women around me felt secure, we wanted to look outwards to make other people feel supported, too. *C'est incroyable.*

That's how the Pink Protest came about, a collective for female activism created by me, Scarlett and two other women I'm completely obsessed with: **Alice** and **Honey**. We wanted to use our platforms to support female-led campaigns. We've worked on various projects helping women and LGBTQ+ people, a campaign ending period poverty being the main one. Period poverty is this very sexist form of poverty where kids can't afford menstrual products and so have to miss school when they're on their periods. There's more information on our website, so I'm not going to try and convince you here. You came for sex, drugs and salacious gossip. Shame on you.

But the best thing about the Pink Protest is that it is sort of the embodiment of everything I care about, and working on it means working with women who represent all those things.

I mean, Alice (Skinner) did the cover for this book, which is probably the main reason you bought it, isn't it? So essentially our female friendship is the reason you have this book. That's pretty cool. That's the power of female friendship, and that's what men are scared shit-less of.

When I have my periodic breakdowns and I think that I'm a terrible person that no one likes, my mum always says the same thing to me. 'Grace,' she'll say, 'I have never met someone with a group of more fiercely loyal and loving friends. So you're definitely getting something right.'

I am so proud of the friendships I've nurtured, that I know are going to be with me forever. Of course I have failed at some friendships, which is sad, but the ones I have now, I'm so proud of. If everything else in my life fails, I will always have the girls and my sunglasses.

Maybe you're thinking, 'But Grace, where's the shame? Where's my "lesson" about what this has taught you about shame?' This chapter isn't about shame, get over it. This is about why you should be so fucking obsessed with your friends that sometimes you feel like you're going to faint when you're trying to describe what they mean to you. This is about lifting up the other people in your life so much that they also lift you, so that performing a set to ten people isn't daunting. And straight men, I'm talking about you, too. Be obsessed with the people in your life. Rely on them. Let them rely on you. You lot have been getting it wrong for too long and now's the time to make it right.

And while you're recovering from that profound point, let me paint you a picture of the zenith of female friendship.

Audrey and Betty taught me all I needed to know about friendship. Audrey and Betty were the most BFFE people I knew. They were my grandmas. People never believe me when I tell them that my grandmas were best friends. Grandmas are never best friends. In *Meet the Fockers*, the grandmas hate each other. And this is just another classic stereotype that perpetuates the idea that women must always compete with each other. Grandmas can never be best friends because they're too busy trying to be the best grandma.

But this wasn't the case with Audrey and Betty. Audrey and Betty were a team. Their relationship was so pure, it was like a highland spring. Betty was my dad's mum. She was the cutest Scottish woman. She called me 'pet' and said 'wee', and not in the French way! Her hair was always perfectly permed and her breath always smelt like fresh peppermint. Betty was never silent; even if she wasn't speaking, she was humming or singing. Her house was always the warmest, most welcoming place in the world.

Audrey is my mum's mum. She's a funny, straight-to-the-point woman who came from a very working-class family in Hull. Audrey never likes fuss. She's always been very frugal and hates how lavish my mum is. She's an incredible pianist, and if we were at a party with a piano present, Audrey and Betty would always be found leading the music. Audrey playing, Betty singing.

Audrey was widowed when I was born, and ten years later Betty was widowed, too. After this they became especially close.

When Betty would come down to visit us, she and Audrey would go galivanting around town. Two old gals on the 24 bus down to Leicester Square, then to the ICA, then they'd have a cup of tea somewhere, but they'd never spend more than £1.50 on it – and even if they did, they'd bitch about how overpriced it was. They were like a walking, talking price-comparison app. All they did was talk about how expensive everything was now. They grew up in very different times, before World War Two, without technology as we know it today, and that's what connected them. They were the only ones in our family who could remember what the world used to be like.

Because of this they both looked at the world with fascination. Everything felt new to them, and they spoke about it constantly. They spoke all the time. Whenever I hung out with them, I felt like a third wheel that didn't really have a place in the conversation, because, well, you had to be there, and I wasn't – in the war, and so on.

As I watched Audrey and Betty sustain this friendship well into their eighties, all I wanted to know was that when I'm in my eighties, and my partner is either dead, divorced or making our drinks, my female friendships would still be that strong.

I want to know that in decades to come, I'll be plotting with Scarlett about which member of the patriarchy to overthrow.

That I will still be taking weed gummies with Anna, and hysterically laughing about how wrinkly our tits are now.

I want to know that one day Tyler and I will live together again. Like *Grace and Frankie*. We'll stay up late talking shit about our ex-lovers, eating tacos and smoking vapes.

'I'm gonna go off for a wank,' I'll say to Tyler.

'Okay, babes, just make sure you don't get up too fast like last time. I can't be fucked to do another trip to A&E tonight.'

IF JEALOUSY IS A SIN THEN INFLUENCER CULTURE IS TAKING US ALL TO HELL

I **wake up** on Monday morning, as usual two hours late. Every Monday I ambitiously set my alarm for 7.30 a.m. And another for 7.31, 7.36, 7.40, 7.55, 8, 8.15, 8.20 and 8.30. But my subconscious knows I need sleep, so she turns them off without me knowing.

When I eventually stir, I realise my sheets are soggy because I've sweated through my skin. My bedroom smells like alcoholic salt. I check the time. Fuck. I have a to-do list the size of Mark Wahlberg's morning routine.

I'm still hungover from Saturday. On Saturday, me and the girls had one of our classic days out. It started wholesome, but it was bound to escalate into a bender because it always does. We started in a pub in Finsbury Park – me, Anna, Jack, Tara, Emily, Holly and Jess – watching an Arsenal match and pretending we cared when Arsenal missed (it is Finsbury Park, so you have to pretend even if you don't care). But we are much more preoccupied with bitching about our boyfriends and taking tequila shots before we'd even had breakfast. Then we decided to go and get our nails done. We drink gin-and-tonic cans while we are sitting in the boiling-hot nail shop getting our acrylics done.

We then move to another pub in Finsbury Park – by this point, we are completely smashed. Daytime drinking is the best kind of drinking and one of our favourite hobbies. Then Bae arrives. He isn't fazed by how obnoxiously loud and aggressive the girls and I are when we're all together. We go quickly from assassinating each other's characters to descending into a fight to being completely obsessed with each other, and as a spectator, it's like an episode of *The Real Housewives of Beverly Hills*. In our heads, we have our own reality show: *The Fucked Women of Finsbury Park*.

Now I'm on tequila lime sodas, then Bae buys me a shot of coffee Patrón. I take it, and then need a shit suddenly. I run to the toilet. Anna and Tara are already in there, so I push in the queue – soz guys. They are also doing poos, so we stank that toilet out. When we are washing our hands we start being each others cheerleaders. I'm telling them how proud I am of them – Tara's a full-time secondary-school teacher who's got her shit together and Anna's just started an amazing new job. A sober-looking girl in the toilet queue says, 'Can you lot get out of here, you're holding everyone else up.' We all turn and glare at her, ready for a fight, until we clock that she is right; we are hogging the toilet space, so we leave.

When we get back upstairs, the pub is really busy all of a sudden. Bae and Anna have gone to the bar to get me a drink. I sit down. Now I know I am smashed because I am watching Bae and Anna talking, talking, talking, and I am jealous that they are leaving me out. 'Get a grip,' Jack said.

'That's your best friend and your boyfriend – be happy that they love each other.'

Still, I storm over. 'WHY ARE YOU LEAVING ME OUT?' I shout at them. They both start laughing, because they can see the level of drunk I am.

'You asked us to get you a drink, Grace,' Anna says.

I realise I am being irrational, so I say, 'Well, blame Tony Blair for my jealousy.' They laugh, but it is true. It's because of him that I am in a pub in Finsbury Park, fucked off my face, getting angry at my boyfriend and best friend for talking. Anyone who tells me otherwise is a terrible person who eats raw beef for breakfast.

Rapidly, we forget about my moment. We go outside for a cigarette, and someone passes me a hash spliff. I smoke a bit and then remember that I fucking hate being high. A fight breaks out between some Arsenal fans next to us. We spectate as they sloppily miss every punch. Eventually it gets broken up and the two men hug intimately, then go back in and make up over another pint.

Finally, the night ends up at Rowans. If you've ever lived in North London, you'll know the establishment Rowans. It's a bowling alley/arcade/night club in Finsbury Park. We've been going there for years. I got banned when I was twenty-one. I can't tell you why; it's between Rowans and me. Plus I like creating mysteries when I can. But now, after months of writing to Rowans, on this day when we happen to be out in Finsbury Park, they replied saying, 'The Grace Campbell Ban has been lifted.'

So we march to Rowans to celebrate my new liberty. The drinks there are cheap – worryingly so. I sometimes wonder if they are what they're supposed to be because I'm always sick when I go there. We go to the smoking area because the DJ is playing a remix of Justin Bieber's 'Baby'. The next few hours fly by as we do shots of bootleg tequila and drink piss-weak beer. A man spills his drink down Anna's back when we are at the bar, and we get into a fight with him because he refuses to apologise. Jack and Bae come over and defuse the situation. Then I suddenly feel hungry, and Bae and I leave. When we get home we order pizza (one meat supreme and one veggie supreme) but fall asleep before it arrives.

On Sunday I am sort of hungover but still a bit drunk and delirious, so Bae and I lie in bed all day having hungover sex while *Stranger Things* plays in the background. That night Bae has to leave because he has to go to his place and get his stuff for work in the morning.

So on Monday, the hangover really kicks in. I wake up alone, like a sad little lost pigeon who flew too far from Trafalgar Square. I'm hugging a pillow like it's my last chance at self-esteem. I have so much work to do, but because I have nowhere to go, I tell myself my bed is my desk, so I stay, lying in my desk for as long as my bladder will let me.

I turn my phone off Airplane Mode and go straight to my lover: Instagram. Unconsciously, I start scrolling through Instagram stories, watching them like they're BBC news. Then I see that a girl I know is on her way to LA. This is a girl I met at a party a few months ago, and she has the career I want. She's funny, fashionable and a writer. She's also flying business class. Ugh. I wanna be flying business class. I feel nauseous. 'Omg, so amazing!' I reply to her.

Then I go onto her profile as a form of competitive self-harm. I'm like a binge-eater, and my food is gorgeous, successful women's Instagram profiles. I see she's got 50,000 more followers than me. This makes me anxious. She's probably going to go to LA, get commissioned to make a show for Netflix and become so rich that I'll eventually have to work for her as her dog-walker.

Then I click on another girl who's commented on one of her pictures. She's a businesswoman, and she's also insanely buff, and has a huge house in London and an adorable puppy. She's so rich. I see she's done a podcast with a model. I go on the model's profile. She's posted a picture with Gigi Hadid. From there I go on Gigi Hadid's profile. Wow, she's so buff. So rich. She must be so happy. I see she's hanging out with Dua Lipa. This tips me over the edge.

I feel unhealthy, I feel slow and I feel butters. I'm also not hitting any of my career goals. My New Year's resolution this year was to make £100,000; it's June and I've made no money. Oh, and what's that? I can feel a cold sore coming.

I start to blame myself. Why do I just go out and get pissed all the time? I bet people like Dua Lipa don't do that. I decide to go and look at someone's profile who will make me feel better. Who will make me feel better? Oh yes, there's a girl I know who now has three children and usually when I look at her profile I remember how lucky I am to be so free and childless. But then, when I get onto her profile, I see that her and her adorable family are in Whitstable, and they're staying in an amazing house on the beach with shutters and a hot tub, and in the self-timer family portrait they've taken they look like they love each other so much. Fuck. Why don't I have three kids?

I go back to the homepage and someone I know has just posted about wanking. This annoys me. Wanking is my thing. Is this girl trying to copy me? Then I remember I didn't invent wanking, and I wasn't the first person to talk about it, but this girl, she's jarring me. I can hear Scarlett's voice in my head telling me to stop, 'Grace, you are so incredible, don't compare yourself to them,' she's saying, but I'm on a tirade and I won't stop until my sense of self is like a piece of dog shit on the heath being eaten by another dog.

I see that someone else I know is on holiday in the Caribbean with her partner. I want to be on holiday in the Caribbean with my partner. I want her body. I want her flat stomach and her perfect tits and her perfect white teeth and her silky hair and I want her fucking life.

I lock my phone. Stop this now. Get in the shower. You have your own work to do. I get in the shower and play Fleetwood Mac loud enough for the neighbours to hear. I'm being dramatic because in the shower I start crying in the hope that I make this a movie moment. But it's not like a movie. The reasons I am crying are both irrational and chemically induced.

I get out of the shower and call Bae, who is on his way to work. I tell him I've done it again: 'I got lost in an Instagram hole. I just started looking at all of these women who are just so much more buff and successful than me.' In the eighteen months we've been together, he's become used to these moments.

'Remember, you're amazing, Gracie. You're funny and everyone you know loves you.' I stop crying.

'Promise me everyone loves me?'

'Of course, all of your friends love you.'

'And do they think I'm the funniest person they know?'

'Sure they do. You are hilarious, and you're going to be so successful. Just maybe don't look at Instagram again today?'

We hang up the phone. He's right. I should avoid Instagram today. That's what I'll do. I'll have an Instagram-free day. But then I start thinking about the fact that Bae is going to work. He works with other women. I remember a stat Emily once told me: that 30 per cent of relationships start at work. He's probably going to fall in love with someone at work. I have to go there. I have to stop it. Then I remember how much he loves me. We just had the best weekend. Don't ruin it, Grace. I climb off that ladder. While I do my hair, I start thinking about what I could do in the mornings instead of going on Instagram. If only I was a grown-up who switched on Radio 4 when she woke up. Maybe I should start the day listening to the *Today* programme. I always think people who do that are really grown up. But I'm never even up early enough to hear it. And then I remember that the world is absolute chaos and that hearing about that first thing in the morning would also stress me the fuck out.

However, at least they're real things happening. I should be affected by climate change and the refugee crisis. If I wasn't then I'd basically be a Tory. I shouldn't be crying in the shower about some girl I met once who's going to LA . . .

She was flying business class, though.

I sit down to work at my kitchen table. I check my emails. There are so many, and yet none of them are filling me with hope. Just people reminding me of things I need to do: admin, admin, admin – it makes me anxious. Then I see that my mum has emailed me about an online yoga class that she's just done. The message says: 'Think you'd like this one darling, ly xxxx.' This makes me cry. God, I love my mum so much. How is it possible to love a human being this much? I don't deserve to have her send me yoga classes. She just knows what makes me happy and she always does it. But right now I feel unworthy of her love.

I can't stop crying. Then I remember how, when I was twelve, my brother Rory got his first real girlfriend, Zoe. Zoe was really great and very older-sisterly to me, which was cool. But I was severely jealous of her relationship with my mum. My mum loved having a girl in the house who wasn't a child. Someone she could talk to about Brazilian blow-dries and the Chanel No. 5 sale. I felt left out. The moment I was defeated by this relationship was when my mum started giving Zoe her old clothes. These weren't old vests from H&M. They were very nice pieces of designer clothing and accessories that I had been hoping would be passed down to me one day. This defeated me for two reasons: firstly, I wanted them for myself, and secondly, now at fourteen, I was already much bigger than my mum, and none of them would have even fit me.

Then I start attacking my body. I stare for a long time at my stomach. I can see it growing. No, I'm not doing this. I put a baggy T-shirt on and stop looking in the mirror. But then I remember my mum and how perfect her body is, and how I'll never have a body like hers when I'm in my sixties. Stop attacking your mum, she's your best friend, she's the creator of all things good. Yes, I'm obsessed with her, I love her.

I text Tyler, who lives with me but is currently at work; 'I'm bugging out ty. Like, literally having crazy irrational thoughts.'

She replies instantly, 'Oh babes. Love you. It's probs because you're still reeling from the weekend. Have a day off today? Watch something that makes you happy? I'll be home this evening, and we can watch something trashy.'

I'm not convinced having a day off will make me feel better. There's nothing I can watch right now. If I watch a good comedy, I'll be jealous that I didn't make it. And I can't watch anything that isn't comedy because I'm too volatile to process death, violence or another period drama. I decide to do the yoga class my mum sent me. It's a slow and gentle class. I need my mind to be slow and gentle. Afterwards, I do feel slightly better. I go on Instagram one more time that day, and as soon as I get on there I feel furious again. I have to get out of here today. I leave Instagram and delete the app.

When Tyler comes home she finds me plucking my nipple hairs and watching *Grace and Frankie* in bed. 'Pasta parcels?' she asks. (You might know this as tortellini.)

I jump up. All I've eaten today are Mini Cheddars with blocks of Cheddar. *J'adore*, but not good for the insides.

'Ty, I've been having a breakdown all day.' I sing the next part: 'I'm never gonna be the person I want to be.' This makes her laugh.

'Babe, you've already done so much. What are you talking about?? Look, you're honestly just having an insecure day. We all have them, but I promise you it's your anxiety speaking. You need a good night's sleep.'

'I'm scared I won't be able to sleep again.' I'm still plucking my nipple hairs.

'Your nipples are huge,' she says.

'I know, that's why there's so much hair on them!'

Tyler agrees to sleep with me that night. She falls asleep straight away, holding my hand, and hearing her sleeping next to me while my mind is being the opposite of slow and gentle makes me feel guilty. I'm so lucky. I've got so many people who worry about me. Why am I stressing them all out? They're all gonna leave me. Tyler will go eventually. My mum. What would I do without her? But they love me. That's why they're all still here. Everyone loves me. Tyler's fast asleep in my bed, holding my clammy, anxious hand. She loves me.

•

I wake up the next day the better version of me. The version of me who is obsessed enough with myself that I can be happy for other people's portrayals of joy on social media.

I'm not always a jealous person. But unfortunately, my insecurities mean I have a habit of comparing myself to other people like a car dealer compares Mini Coopers to Beetles. I weigh up what I've got vs other people, and then, when I lose my grip on myself, my insecurities turn comparisons into jealous rages.

When my mental health is good, the rational side of my head – the voice of reason – is loud. It reminds me that no one is trying to ruin my life and that I am a wonderful person. But when my mental health is on a downward spiral, my head turns into a writers' room, and my insecurities are the writers. They're writing the script of my life, and they're writing themselves into well-thought-through storylines that I believe. Storylines with a sense of impending doom. The doom being that I will eventually be a failure.

You might be able to relate to this, because, honestly, in this climate? Are you fucking kidding me? How is it possible to not be jealous of other people? Every time you go online, you're putting yourself at risk of feeling jealous of someone else and their supposedly perfect life. I don't think we should suppress these feelings. I think, when jealousy arrives, we should say hi and ask why it's here. We should listen, and then we should show it the door before it gets involved in our personal business.

As you can see, I have become very mature and know how to deal with jealousy – I'm now totally cured of that demon feeling. Just yesterday I found out how much one of my friends is earning in her new job and I was just so purely happy for her. No part of me considered becoming an estate agent. I definitely didn't consider getting an Only Fans account.

No – for real, like hay fever, my jealousy still flares up. But the one thing I know how to do now is not to stay in an Instagram hole for so long that it eventually feels like a k-hole.

TIMES WHEN I MIGHT EXPERIENCE JEALOUSY

- When someone tells me they've read a book on capitalism.

- When Anna gets a tan after five minutes in the sun.

- When my parents go on holiday without me, 'as a couple'.

- When I find out my friends have a WhatsApp group that I'm not in.

- Every year when the BAFTA nominations come out and I haven't been nominated. (I've never made anything that could be nominated.)

- When I find out someone else is having more sex than me.

- When someone I don't like has more Instagram followers than me.

- When someone I do like has more Instagram followers than me.

- When I meet someone who speaks multiple languages but doesn't brag about it.

- Every time my boyfriend talks to anyone who isn't me (including my mum).

- If my boyfriend gets a haircut and sees other people before he sees me.

- When my dad speaks to another woman who isn't my mum.

- Each time I remember that my therapist sees other clients that aren't me.

- When someone I know gets a modelling job as a side hustle.

- When someone the same age as me has kids and a dog.

- When someone the same age as me is single and happy and making a lot of money.

- When someone the same age as me has a mortgage and a car that they don't share with their mum.

- When someone at a party is more drunk than me.

- When someone at a party is more sober than me.

- When I looked at my mum's passport and saw that I wasn't the number to call in an emergency.

THE BREAKUP LETTER

In my life, I've spent a lot of time being jealous of how much attention my parents gave to politics. But I don't hate politics as a whole. In fact, as I've gotten older, I've spent lots of my mental energy worrying about politics. And in particular, worrying about the Labour Party. How could I not? My whole life has been about it.

Did you know that my full name is *Grace Iona Rose Campbell*? Cool name, right? Well, even my name was determined by Labour. I was named Grace after Grace Gould, the child of Philip Gould, one of the key strategists for New Labour, and Gail Rebuck, a very successful British business woman who is now a Labour Peer. My middle name is Iona, because that's where John Smith, Tony Blair's predecessor, was buried. My other middle name is Rose, because . . . wait for it . . . the New Labour logo was a rose. 'Count yourself lucky,' my dad used to say. 'If you'd been born pre-rose, you'd be called Grace Red Flag Campbell.' (Labour's old logo.) Honestly, imagine if my middle name was Red Flag! No one would want to talk to me. Anyway, I'm currently in the process of changing my middle name by deed poll to Rosé, as a distancing tactic from the Labour Party. *J'adore le rosé* more than the Labour Rose.

Anyway, in the last decade, the Labour Party has been slowly splitting into two parts. I actually think we should call it the Labia Party, because it's more like a labia now. It has two flaps. The left flap was led by Jeremy Corbyn and his closest ally, John McDonnell, and there was the right flap: that was my dad, Toothy Tony and David Miliband. Clearly, somebody needed to bring the flaps back together, and I wanted that someone to be me.

In 2016, when Jeremy Corbyn was the Labour Party leader and the split was really starting to appear, my dad got asked to go on *Question Time*, the BBC's political debating show. My dad called me up one day and said, 'Listen, Grace, I've been asked to go on *Question Time* with John McDonnell, and I'm scared I'm gonna punch him in the face, so I need you to come with me to make sure I don't.'

John McDonnell was the Shadow Chancellor of the Exchequer at the time, and as I've mentioned, one of Corbyn's closest pals in the Labia. My dad was inviting me along to *Question Time* because he knows that when I'm there, the chances of him getting into a fight with McDonnell will be slimmer, because he hates fighting in front of his kids. That's the kind of calm and gentle soul my dad is.

And who knew that at *Question Time* an opportunity for me to mend the Labia would arise? We were in the green room before the show. There were some very plain egg-and-cress sandwiches on a platter, which I was wolfing down along with a Diet Coke. Then John McDonnell comes in. McDonnell is a small man, and it's not that he looks like a snake, but on first impressions, he gave me very strong serpent vibes. As you know, I'm very protective of my dad, so I stood in front of him and started growling with my eyes. And then all of a sudden my anger dissipated, because I noticed that behind McDonnell was a tall, just-above-average-looking boy, and all I wanted to do was get to know him.

He was John McDonnell's special advisor – or SPAD, in the politics world. And when the show begins, McDonnell's SPAD and I go and sit in the gallery to watch the debate. We're not sitting with the crowd – we're a balcony up, and we've got the whole thing to ourselves. *Romantique.*

I turn to him and say, 'What's your name?' and I congratulate myself for being so flirtatious.

'Seb,' he says.

'And so, Seb . . . when did you start working for ~~my~~ the Labour Party?' Wow watch me flirt.

'Well,' he says, 'when my dad won, I came back from Venezuela, where I was living, and started working for him.'

I was confused. 'And . . . who is your dad?'

'Jeremy,' he said, like he was telling me his dad was Beyoncé or Madonna. But I was able to do the maths, and when I worked it out, my heart started doing the splits.

'Corbyn?' I asked, cool.

'Yep,' he said. And then I realised my purpose in life. And a quote sprang into my mind. A quote from a man called William Shakespeare. 'Two households, both alike in dignity, in fair North London, where we lay our scene.'

It was obvious to me in that moment that me and Seb Corbyn were the Romeo and Juliet of the Labour Party. This was how I was going to bring the two flaps of the Labia back together ... with the power of my very own labia. Seb started watching the debate, and I began to daydream about our wedding. My dad, and Jeremy, making speeches, hugging. Then Seb and I would go off to Cuba for our honeymoon, where we'd conceive our first child, who Seb would insist we called Fidel. I was buzzing.

But when I snapped out of my daydream, I looked back at Seb and I could see he was stressed. I'd been so preoccupied thinking about which tartan I would wear on our wedding day that I hadn't listened to any of the debate. When I looked down, I could see that my dad and John McDonnell were properly beefing. They were shouting at each other, and the other panellists were looking amused by this scene. I tuned in just when McDonnell called my dad 'nauseating'. Sorry ... what? That little serpent puppet/ Seb's boss/Seb's dad's best friend had just called MY dad nauseating?

I realised that my dad and McDonnell might just have cockblocked Seb and me. But also, was I just fantasising about this guy because I saw the potential to use him to mend the Labour Party? Was that how deep my obsession with politics went, that I would marry someone to try to mend the party that I was named after?

After the debate, Seb and I walked back to the green room in silence. I was nervous to see what vibe we'd find when we got in there. I knew I'd walk in to find some real tension between my dad and McDonnell, but what I found was much more than that.

I walked in to find McDonnell in a corner with my dad leaning over him, clenching his fist and shouting, 'You and yours are about to fuck up the Labour Party forever.' His vein was popping out from the left side of his neck. That's his angry vein. He's gonna punch him! What do I do? I pulled my dad away from the puppet. I forgot about Seb completely.

'You two are pathetic!' I shout. 'You couldn't even pretend for an hour that you can get along. You're an embarrassment to Labour.' And then ... I heard someone slow-clapping. I thought, 'Is that Seb?' No, couldn't be. I could see that Seb's hands were perfectly still. I turned around, and David Dimbleby, the host of *Question Time*, was at the door, giving me a round of applause. Media acclaim. I liked it.

The whole experience made me realise that I don't want to use my precious energy trying to mend the Labour Party. Right now, you can probably see that British politics is falling apart – a bit like the last flat-pack Ikea chair I sat on.

I've spent many restless nights lying awake, wishing there was something I could do to make it better. But now, I'm done with it. I'm done feeling like I owe politics my mental power – or my vagina power. I think this has been a long time coming.

When I was fifteen years old, somebody slyly took a picture of me smoking a spliff at a house party. They then sent said picture to the *Sun* newspaper. Do you know the *Sun*? Rupert Murdoch both produces and wipes his very wrinkly arse with it. So the *Sun* had this picture of me smoking a spliff. I don't even think it was a spliff – it was just a terrible roll-up – but anyway, whoever took it I guess thought it would be ammunition to have a go at my dad . . .

As it turned out, the *Sun* didn't publish the picture because I was underage. But after this whole episode, my mum sat me down and said, 'Grace, you can't be reckless with this stuff. You'll never be able to have a career in politics if it comes out that you take drugs.' And I must say, for a moment that made me want to take drugs even more, if it meant that I could write off a career in politics.

But this did make me paranoid. I felt there was a lot riding on me not fucking up. Firstly, I really didn't want to fuck up the reputation of my school, which Dua Lipa and I (and the teachers, yes, they were great) were doing so much to build. I knew the media would love to paint the picture of Alastair Campbell's daughter as a state-school stoner, so I had to be on my guard. My friends were, as ever, loyally protective of me. We took this event very seriously and upped the ante on the question of who we trusted to be around us. This type of thing never happened again.

You might be thinking, what does this have to do with my relationship with politics? And what does that have to do with shame? Well, the tabloids in particular have always felt like a scary Dementor in my life. I guess I am giving them more ammo than a spliff with this book. I mean, I know that you, lovely reader, can also see the lovely person I am, but I am sure you know enough about the tabs to understand that from what's in this book alone they could paint me as a drug-addicted, sex-crazed, permanently fanny-farting, frankly perverted, nasty, jealous woman who is chronically and tragically obsessed with Dua Lipa. They love any excuse to print a picture of Dua, as do I.

The chances are they won't say any of that stuff about me, because most of their readers don't know who I am. However, if I ever made the decision to go into politics, the papers would sure as hell make sure they knew me, and they have plenty of good/bad info to hand, provided by my very own pen. It is not that this is what deters me from ever doing it, but rather that I don't really want to work in a political environment where publications like that have so much say in how you are projected to the outside world.

And then there's the trolls. I'm not even a politician, but I have lots of trolls on the Internet who like to hate on me as though I was. I've had trolls giving me whatever the opposite of constructive criticism is since I was fourteen years old. These are trolls who @ me either because they don't like my dad, don't like women or don't like accounts that haven't got the Union Jack in their handle.

These trolleys, as I now call them, have said all kinds of things to me. Hundreds have told me I'm 'repulsive', or 'hideous', or a 'fat man'. I have one trolley who repeatedly comments on pictures of me and my dad, and calls me his 'son'. Very often I am told I look like Mick Hucknall, but that one I've taken as a compliment, because I remember reading an article in *Heat* once that said he'd slept with over 1,000 women.

Truthfully, I don't think my anxiety could handle being in politics. It's one thing being a woman with an opinion on the Internet. Even then, people are either waiting for you to fuck up so they can call you out or, usually bots, are insulting you every second of the day in the hope that you'll eventually implode and vow never to have an opinion ever again.

But then there's being a woman with an opinion in a position of power on the Internet. Women in politics get abuse hurled at them online all the time, because the country is full of men who still can't accept that women now have real power. And then there's the issue of racism. Did you know that 50 per cent of all abuse directed towards female MPs is directed at Diane Abbott? She was Britain's first Black female MP, and has been an MP since 1987, which is a huge deal. There are over 220 women MPs, and 50 per cent of all hate online is directed towards one Black woman. Now, I know that the abuse directed at Abbott is both racist and sexist, and I couldn't compare a white woman's experience online to hers. But what does it say about this country, that people are so unable to handle a Black woman being in a position of power that they need to try to tear her down? That they will harass her in the hope that they can push her into not wanting to be in power any more? The Internet allows the worst type of abuse to fester, and I'm afraid a lot of that abuse is directed towards women in positions of power.

And I have, in recent years, realised that politics is not the only way to change the world. Those in power are being upstaged a bit at the moment by young people. You've heard of Greta, yes? How cool is that? Only seventeen and known the world over by her first name, like Britney. But Britney doesn't have her own Generation named after her. Generation Greta is much more than Greta T, but what it means is that there is a whole generation of young people who are rejecting actual politics and changing the world in other ways.

Now, obviously this generation has been going since long before Greta hit the scene. I've actually had a part in this. Not Greta Thunberg levels, because she is a teenage icon. But with the Pink Protest, I have been part of a movement that has been galvanising young people. Scarlett and I even organised a protest for Amika George, the teenage activist, and her #freeperiods campaign, which ended up changing the government's laws on period poverty in the UK. So obviously, politics, we do need you, because that change wouldn't have happened without you. But we don't all need to be inside you. Gross. That sounds sexual. I certainly don't want any of them inside me.

So now, as Frank Sinatra puts it, the end is near . . . it is time for the break-up letter.

Dear Politics,

This is not easy for either of us. We go so far back. You've given me some of the best moments, and some of the worst. But firstly, I hope you know that I really care about you, and I always have. Even in 2003, I just wanted you to be okay.

It's just that, well, I've become so used to you holding a huge space in my life, and I realised recently that our relationship has become a bit toxic.

Now, I'm not perfect, you know that, and I never want people to think I'm on the moral high ground, because I am always completely transparent about my flaws. But you make me feel that I have to be perfect. All the time. You make me feel like there's no room for mistakes or admitting you got something wrong, and I don't like that about you.

The breakup letter

I don't like the hold you have over me and my family. I don't like that I can be having a good day, getting my acrylic nails done, and then I read something about another twat who works for you doing or saying something stupid, and I become so angry that I can't even appreciate my new ombré nails.

I don't like that, right now, you're full of men called Boris and Jacob and Toby who all went to the same schools and still think they're there. The worst type of men. And I don't know why you're not doing more to change that.

This is the saddest break-up letter I've ever had to write. Well, actually it's the only break-up letter I've ever had to write, so far. But here we are. It's over, hasta la vista, ciao, we're going our own way. This doesn't have to be forever. There will always be a place in my heart for you. But I don't like you the way you are now. I want you to change, and then perhaps I'll consider coming back to you.

In the meantime, I'm on the shortlist for a new role as Greta Thunberg's joke writer. I have sent her my CV and a new joke, just for her, about Fanny Farts being the new Wind Power. I am planning to get the first Nobel Prize for Comedy. Beat that, Johnson.

Anyway, gotta go now. Sending love, always.

Grace Iona Rosé Campbell

Xxx

THE
DISGRACEFUL CLUB

28 November 2019. I start the day right. With an earth-moving orgasm that's so loud it wakes up everyone on my road. You're welcome. Bae and I like to have sex in the morning when we can, because . . . why not? I shower, have an oat-milk latte and at 9 a.m. I leave to go into town for a mitting. Remember mittings? Invented by Tyler and me.

I love that feeling, of going out to do something serious right after you've been pumped. Don't you? Being on the Tube and still feeling the juice inside you, or smelling the sweaty sex fumes on your skin, just waiting for a stranger, a woman, to look at you with an approving glance to say, 'I know what that smug face means, I see you.' And then, just like that, you're completely validated.

That's the kind of mood I'm in today. I hop onto the packed Northern Line via Charing Cross at Belsize Park. I want to shout, 'Hey, commuters! Apologies for that sex that you smell, *c'est moi!*'

I am meeting with a production company based in Soho, which I'm doing some work with at the moment. There are four other people at this mitting. All of them are older than me. Before the chat really kicks off, I'm sitting at the table, looking around, and I imagine that everyone else here was also having an earth-moving orgasm just over an hour ago. I don't go into details in my mind, because I don't want to imagine their cum faces and then have to control my laughter. But just the thought that they, too, might have just had an orgasm makes me feel deeply connected to them.

The mitting goes incredibly well, which I assume is because we've all started the day right. I leave the mitting, and when I'm walking back to the Tube I feel grateful that my orgasms are back. Over the summer, while I was at the Edinburgh Fringe, I lost my orgasm. It was an awful turn of events. I just lost it. One minute I had my orgasm, there, in my hand, and the next, it was gone, and I was sure it had ghosted me. Gone forever.

This had happened because I had just gone back on antidepressants; citalopram, which is a medication I was taking for my anxiety and intrusive thoughts. One of the side effects of citalopram, and most serotonin boosters, is that you can lose your orgasm. Usually this only happens at the beginning, and then afterwards it comes back. But when I lost my orgasm, I was sure it was on the pile of things that were gone from me forever. It was off somewhere, with my Vivienne Westwood purse that was stolen at a party, my six phones that I lost in the summer of 2015 and my faith in British politics. Gone, never to come back.

I was so angry that the doctor had forgotten to tell me that this was a side effect of citalopram. Perhaps they weren't aware of my work, and that my personal brand is very reliant on being able to orgasm. When I lost my orgasm, I thought my career was over. I should have gotten my orgasms insured, like J-Lo did for her bum and Dolly Parton did for her tits.

So there I was, up at the Edinburgh Fringe, doing jokes on stage about sex and wanking, like a complete fraud. This ruined my sense of self. But I knew that the reason I was on this medication was more important than the fact that I wasn't able to come for a bit.

After a month or so, with patience and some very artistic fingering by Bae, I was born again. The orgasm was back.

I'm nearly back at the Tube, as I'm reliving this moment of my summer, when a thought pops into my head. I remember something that a supposed friend of mine said. We were at the pub, just after I'd started taking this medication, right before I was going to Edinburgh, and I told her I had gone on citalopram. I told her I was concerned that the bad, intrusive thoughts I was having might jeopardise my mental health at Edinburgh.

'Oh no, Grace!' she said. 'Why are you going on antidepressants? You seem so happy.' It was obvious she wasn't listening to me. 'You know, we don't even know what's in those pills. I've heard the government puts stuff in them that we don't know about.'

Remembering this moment while I'm walking along Dean Street riles me the fuck up. When I told her about my decision to go on medication, I wasn't asking for her approval. I knew my decision was the right one, because I was the one in my head. I knew what was needed. I didn't really want to hear her opinion, and especially not some conspiracy theory that her cousin's friend's aunt told her about how a pill which is working wonders for me is actually a way for the government to control me.

I'm at the Tube. And I'm relieved remembering that my orgasm is back and my mental health is doing better. I'm still on the medication, and it really has made me so much happier, so I won't let some anti-vaxxer who still goes on Facebook tell me what's what about medication.

I get on the Tube, and my relief has magically changed again to feeling irritated by how easily affected I am by people's disapproval of me. My Tube carriage is empty, apart from an old man sitting opposite, who reminds me of Ian McKellen. He's wearing a perfectly tailored navy-blue suit, and tucked into his jacket pocket is a mint-green handkerchief. Then I notice that his handkerchief is perfectly matched with his socks. His attention to detail inspires me. I wonder where he's going. Maybe he has a date with an old fling he's trying to win back. Maybe he's going to a luncheon for a charity that he is a patron of, a charity whose main focus is clean water. Wherever he's going, I'm sure he'll be admired.

When I get back to Belsize Park I feel much calmer. I think the energy of that old man was something special. I wish I'd got to thank him. Instead, I wish him a good day in my head, and hope that he receives my thought somehow.

Okay, now I have to get into the zone for tonight. Tonight is a fucking huge deal for me, and probably the reason why I'm in such a manic mood. It is the first ever night of my very own comedy show: *The Disgraceful Club*, a raucous night that is happening at The Box, the infamous club in Soho. *The Disgraceful Club* will be hosted by me, and I've got an incredible line-up of female and LGBTQ+ comedians performing alongside me.

I'm hosting a night at the motherfucking Box. The Box. The first and only time I'd been to The Box before this was when I was eighteen, and Usain Bolt was there, and I got told off for trying to take a picture of him, and then I drank too much tequila and vomited at the bar.

When I get back from the station I go straight to the toilet because I can feel I have the shits, but when I sit down I feel nothing. It's nerves. I remember that nerves are good. Nerves will mean I'm on my toes.

I call Bae and ask him what he's wearing tonight. 'I told you this morning, I'm wearing what I wore to work because I stayed at yours, and I only had one clean shirt,' he says.

'But I want you to wear the green shirt,' I whine.

'Stop trying to control things, Grace,' he says. 'I know you're stressed, but stop trying to control everything else. Okay? I'm gonna be there at seven and you're going to be amazing.'

I want to shout 'THIS IS MY DAY' at him. But I don't. He's right. Put your nerves where they deserve to be. Tonight. At The Box. You're a legend. Okay, no, you're not. This is going to be an absolute disaster.

Jack arrives looking, as ever, as if he's just walked out of a photoshoot in the Nineties. He's wearing a vintage Adidas two-piece with a ripped Chanel T-shirt underneath. 'The Overground was full of idiot hipsters from Dalston. I wanted to trip them all up,' Jack says, and in that moment, I realise that Jack is the younger version of the man I saw on the Tube.

'Oh my God!' I say, 'I saw older you on the Tube today! He looked happy. Your future is looking bright.'

'Thanks, Mystic Meg. Will tonight go well? That's all I care about right now,' Jack says.

Jack's heavily invested in this night. He loves putting on an event, and he's helped me with a lot of creative ideas and styled both of my looks.

Jack puts the outfits out on the bed, then he pours himself a glass of Prosecco and says, 'I'm so excited, but, like, I haven't eaten all day.' He doesn't offer me a glass because he knows I'll say, 'I don't drink before gigs.' Which is true. I never drink before a performance. Well, not since the night that I had three glasses of wine and threw the fourth one towards a man on the front row because he told me I had a camel-toe. That was my second gig. Never again.

So I'm drinking green tea while I watch Jack get the outfits ready. Look one is a dress/jacket that looks like something Margaret Thatcher would have worn if she was a thot. Look two is a slutty Britney Spears: a pink tartan skirt with a see-through mesh pink top. My boobs are visible, and they're loving it. This is, of course, the outfit I choose to open the show.

We take the Tube to Soho because I'm humble, and I'm hoping to bump into the old man coming back from his luncheon so I can thank him for his kind energy. On the Tube I worry that the humidity might jeopardise how perfectly curled my hair is, Jack keeps twisting it. Everyone on the Tube is watching us. Maybe they think I'm famous because I have someone doing my hair on the Northern Line via Charing Cross. But then also, why would I be on the Tube if I was Lady Gaga? Stranger things have happened, I guess.

We get to Tottenham Court Road station and we go up the escalator. I'm afraid of escalators because I always think they're going to eat me up, and now my phobia is flaring up. I'm anxious and I'm on an escalator. Fuck's sake. Jack's talking about a Netflix series he's just watched and is enthusiastically telling me the plot. I can't concentrate on what he's saying. Something about aliens. I hate aliens. Me and my grandma Audrey, we hate aliens.

Now we're coming to the top of the escalator. Jack hits me lightly and says, 'Grace.' I look up and I see him straight away. Tall, pale as a hat from Pizza Express and wearing a hideous worn-out leather jacket that looks like it's a community centre for all moths, Will is tapping his Oyster card on the machine while listening to music and bopping his head like the lame uncle at a party.

Will hasn't seen us. Jack knows Will and dislikes him deeply, and also hates talking to people he bumps into; he doesn't like a conversation that gets thrust upon him. Jack slips behind a woman in front of us who is taking ages to move away from the escalator. He takes my hand and we rush to the ticket barriers.

'He looked like an old lumberjack,' I say as we walk through Soho.

'No,' Jack says, 'he looked like a teacher who had just been fired for inappropriate touching.'

I can't believe he chose today of all days to reappear in my life. If I was alone, I would have thought I was seeing things. Spotting Will from afar, I feel nothing. Well, that's not true – I feel embarrassed. Embarrassed that I've spent so much of my time worrying about what this person who blends into the walls of Totty Court station thinks about me. After a few minutes, he leaves my mind completely, because my life is so much more exciting now.

Jack and I arrive at The Box. It's so weird seeing a club like that when the lights are on. It's a bit like being at school at night. My agents, Daisy and Alice, who have helped me put this whole thing together, are here and they've got

Kettle Chips and hummus to keep us all going. Anna, Scarlett, Tyler, Alice, Emily and Honey arrive. Everyone looks incredible, like Little Mix at the *X Factor* final.

I do a run-through of my grand entrance. The club has a catwalk going through it, so this takes a bit of practice. 'You need to walk slower,' says Anna. 'You look like you've just done a fart and you're running away from it.'

I try it again. Much slower. 'Yep, that's perfect, do it just like that. Soak it in,' Anna says.

My parents FaceTime me as I'm getting ready. They're in France, which is probably for the best, because them being here would make me even more nervous, and I don't want my dad to upstage me tonight, at my feminist gig. 'Darling, you are going to be so good,' my mum says.

'What joke are you opening with?' asks my dad, pretending to be my comedy mentor when really he can't write jokes, he just inspires them. I get off the phone, because I'm busy and they are so needy. They wish they were here. I bet you do, too, reading this. One day, darling, as my mum would say.

Bae arrives. He squeezes me. We all go downstairs and my friends start drinking – I think to calm their nerves. They're nervous because I'm nervous, and I'm nervous because they're nervous. I get ready in the bathroom while Jack fixes my hair and make-up.

Oenone arrives. She's a new friend of mine. I met her because a few months ago she'd invited me onto her podcast. She turned up, and we instantly connected. We sat in my bed for hours, recording the podcast, and talking about our lives. She's impossible to dislike, and has an inspirational style which I admire.

Oenone wanted to get into comedy, so I've offered her to do her first ever comedy set at *The Disgraceful Club* tonight. You've heard about how *tragique* my first gig was, and I don't want other talented women to have to go through that.

I'm warming up now. I'm going through my new material. I'm vaping in the toilets. I'm being high maintenance, probably ... possibly ... definitely. But Jack, Anna and Tyler are here because they accept me for who I am.

Everyone starts to arrive. Hundreds of people, upstairs, at The Box, to see *The Disgraceful Club*. Scarlett comes in. 'There are so many people!!!! It's heaving.' I need to shit – this time it's real. It all comes out at once. The mania that's been triple-jumping around my brain exits my body in one long swoop.

Daisy comes down and finds me in the toilet with Jack. 'You ready?' she says.

•

'Ladies, gentleman and everyone in between ...' I say through a mic at the back of the venue, 'for the first time ever, will you please welcome to the stage your host of *The Disgraceful Club* ... Grace Campbell.'

I dance down the catwalk. Slowly, I can hear Anna saying, soak it up. Yep, this is a moment. This audience is a motherfucking vibe.

Hey, guys, welcome to The Box. This is a pretty exciting night, I'm gonna be honest. The last time I was here I saw a woman pull her whole outfit out of her fanny and put it on.

And that's how I know I belong here . . . because a few weeks ago I actually put a Malteser in my vagina and fanny farted it into – he doesn't want me to say this was him, but – my boyfriend's mouth.

They're absolutely loving this. They're screaming like mad. I can see said Bae hiding behind his friends.

While we're on fanny farting, which is a skill of mine, I once fanny farted so hard my boyfriend's dick came out. And then I was like, at least now he knows what it feels like to get heckled off stage.

I actually did that joke last week at my friend's wedding. She was marrying an American guy, and a lot of people at the wedding were from the States. She'd asked me to do a set at her wedding, but nothing too rude, so I opened the set with that joke, because it's one of my tamer ones. And the reception was more mixed than usual, which I thought was strange.

Anyway, I found out afterwards that this was because Americans call their bum their fanny, so they all thought I was talking about doing anal and shitting my boyfriend's dick out of my arsehole at one of my best friends' wedding. I couldn't believe they thought I'd be that rude.

J'adore.

And I know I've done it. The show is off. I introduce the first act, my pal and fellow Riot Girl Sophie Duker. She smashes it. My friends are laughing so much they keep turning to me when I'm sat with them and mouthing, 'SO good.'

When the break comes, Jack and Anna come backstage and help me change into look two. I can't quite relax yet but in the room downstairs I can feel that everyone around me is happy.

After the break I'm going to do five minutes and then I'll introduce Oenone. Oenone's got it, whatever that is – she's got funny in her bones. I introduce her and tell everyone it's her first ever comedy set. She goes out, and the crowd is so heavenly I want to lick all of their faces. Not long into her set, everyone realises that they don't have to support her because it's her first gig, but because she is phenomenal. She's doing accents, she's telling banging jokes. And I'm watching her, and I'm so happy for her . . . but I'm also a little jealous.

I wish I'd had this as my first gig. How is she this good, and getting this reception, at her first gig? Why am I being bitter?

I catch myself. Shut the fuck up, Grace, you look too good to be having such ugly thoughts in your head. I look around my table of friends. I couldn't do any of the things I'm doing it if weren't for my friends, sitting at this table with me, supporting me in this way.

Then I hear another voice in my head. 'You're a bit of a bitch, Grace Campbell. Jealousy is the last thing you should be feeling right now and you should be ashamed.' And suddenly I was.

But instead of digging in on the hate and jealousy and spiralling down to the places they always take me, I just snap right out of it then and there. This night is a space I've created to support other people, and it has to be totally jealousy free, especially from you, Grace.

And then I feel happy for all the other performers, and happy that Oenone's first gig has been so perfect. And happy for myself that I was also spectacular and have put on this amazing night. I sit and look at all these women around me and they sort of lift up from the floor and dance in front of my eyes with glitter coming out of their vaginas and dildo-shaped stars shooting from their eyes. I'm obsessed with this night.

Reader Acknowledgements

Firstly, I'd like to thank my readers. You've put up with me through a lot in this book, and I'm forever grateful for that. Below are how I hope different readers found this book.

All young women: I would love to think this book made you feel less alone, and that you love me as much as I love you. Also, if you did love this book, do pass it on to other women in your life.

Young man who plays 5-a-side: I hope this book made you uncomfortable. I hope that you realized some truths about yourself and your peers. Hopefully you will feel inspired to share it with your friends and none of you will fall into the dickhead category ever again.

Etonian educated Times reading middle aged man: I really hope you fucking hated this book. I hope you haven't made it to this point, because that's how much you hated it. If so, then at least I'll have gotten that right.

Middle aged woman who reads the Guardian: I hope this book helped you understand your daughter a bit better. Now can you stop bitching at her for liking to get her vagina waxed?!

Hollywood agent: All I will say is my inbox is open and it's warm inside. If you're interested, please get in touch. I'm thinking we should get Peter Capaldi to play my dad?

Actual Acknowledgements

Mum and Dad. Thanks for putting up with all my bullshit. I guess you don't really have a choice, do you? But I do really appreciate how deeply you guys love me. I feel lucky to have that. You always take the time to listen to me, even when I'm talking complete and utter shit. There's not a single problem in the world you can't solve. I love how much you love each other too. 40 years and counting, you guys have taught me so much about love. Thanks for always letting me just be me, as obnoxious and troublesome as that has been at points. Thanks for letting me depend on you a tragic amount. You two are my best friends, and I will continue to crash your holidays for as long as you let me.

Tyler, Anna, Scarlett, Emily, Jack, and Tara, thank you for making sure I've never had to go through anything in my life alone. For being the best friends in the world, through everything. For always making everything in my life a team effort. You've made me feel that any kind of failure isn't bad because it's not failure when we're doing it all together. J'adore you all till the end of the world.

Bae, thank you for dealing with my many meltdowns while writing this book. Without you this book wouldn't have been as raw as it is. The way you supported me through this process made me feel safe enough to let so much of the scariest things about my life out onto the page. I'll be forever grateful for your wisdom, honesty, and gorgeous face. Thank you for loving me as much as you have. Love you forever.

Alice Skinner, thank you for your friendship, and your incredible art. Without your cover and illustrations this book wouldn't be as amazing as it is. You are a gorgeous, talented, queen and I can't wait to continue world dominance with you.

To the rest of my family; all of the Millars and the Campbells, my two clans. My brothers Rory and Calum, for supporting me even when they don't really get what it is that I do. To Audrey and Betty, the feminist powerhouses. Donald and Bob, who we miss very much. To Georgia and Grace Gould, and Gail Rebuck, for being my honorary family, and inspiring me always. And to Philip, who I know would have loved this book.

Through my childhood, teenage years, and 20s, I have been supported by an incredible group of friends. Leo, Nina, Ella, Oenone, Holly, Daisy, Sissy, Sophia, Honey, Lulu, Remi, Rhiannon, Kazia, Harriet, Grace, Jess, Red, and so many more.

To Alice Russell and Daisy Janes and the whole team at Found. My life significantly improved when you two arrived into it, and I thank you so much for being the encouraging forces behind me doing this book. Thank you for also being great friends to me as well as my managers. You both do way more than what's in your job description, I'm forever indebted to you.

To my amazing editor, Harriet, without whom this book would have been a ranting mess. From the get go, you got what I was trying to do and you helped me form my life, and my thoughts, into an actual fucking book! It's crazy that we made this book happen during a global pandemic and a lockdown, with many zoom calls where you always assured me that I wasn't doing this alone. I can't thank you enough for your patience, and consistent levels of calm. And to everyone else at Hodder Studio, thank you for being part of this with me, and for welcoming me into this exciting family.

And finally, to all of the dickheads who have ever rejected me. Without you I wouldn't have had such a strong fire in my belly to prove you all wrong. I wish you nothing but diarrhea.